CW01648633

MADEIRA HIKING GUIDE 2025 - 2026

Top Trails, hidden routes and scenic treks for every skill level

Miller Pharr

All right, reserve 2025

No part of this book may be reproduced, distributed, or transmitted in any form or by any means, including photocopying, recording, or other electronic or mechanical methods, without the prior written permission.

Table of Contents

Introduction to Madeira 3

Planning Your Trip 14

Budgeting for Your Hiking Adventure 23

Essential Gear and Packing Guide 32

Top Hiking Trails in Madeira 40

Seasonal Hiking and Weather Considerations 54

Hiking Safety and Emergency Preparedness 61

Local Culture, Food and Activities 66

Festivals, Events, and Local Hiking Calendar 70

Environmental Responsibility and Hiking Ethics .. 78

Practical Travel Tips 83

Recommended Itineraries 88

Resources and Further Reading 98

Final Thoughts 102

Downloadable Map. *107*

Chapter 1

Introduction to Madeira

The island of Madeira, a volcanic gem rising from the vast Atlantic Ocean, is one of the most breathtaking hiking destinations in the world. Located off the northwest coast of Africa and part of Portugal, this rugged yet lush paradise is renowned for its dramatic cliffs, deep valleys, and ancient forests. Madeira's landscape is a striking blend of towering peaks, misty laurel forests, and coastal trails that seem to hover above the ocean. Madeira is more than just a destination for those who love the outdoors—it's an immersive experience where nature, history, and adventure come together in perfect harmony.

1.1 Overview of Madeira as a Hiking Destination

Hiking in Madeira is unlike anywhere else in the world. The island's unique geography—formed by volcanic activity millions of years ago—has created an awe-inspiring terrain of steep ridges, high-altitude plateaus, and deep-cut valleys. Trails snake through these landscapes, offering hikers a chance to traverse everything from cloud-covered mountain peaks to levada paths that follow ancient irrigation channels through dense forests.

One of Madeira's most distinctive features is its levadas—a network of narrow water channels built to distribute water from the high mountains to farmland below. These levadas, many of which date back centuries, have become some of the island's most famous hiking routes. Following these pathways leads visitors through lush Laurisilva forests, past waterfalls, and into the heart of Madeira's untouched wilderness. This ancient laurel forest, a UNESCO World Heritage Site, is a living relic of the Tertiary period, home to rare plants and bird species found nowhere else on Earth.

The island's diverse hiking trails cater to every level of experience. Beginners can enjoy leisurely walks along the levadas, shaded by a canopy of green, while experienced hikers can challenge themselves on rugged mountain routes, such as the exhilarating Pico do Arieiro to Pico Ruivo trail, which connects Madeira's two highest peaks. The sheer variety of landscapes—from black volcanic cliffs plunging into the Atlantic to the serene, wind-swept plateaus of Paul da Serra—ensures that every hike offers a new and unforgettable experience. Beyond its landscapes, Madeira's climate makes it a year-round hiking paradise. Thanks to its subtropical location and the influence of the Gulf Stream, temperatures remain mild throughout the year. Even in the heart of winter, the island rarely experiences extreme cold, and in summer, cooling ocean breezes prevent the heat from becoming overwhelming. This means hikers can explore Madeira's trails any time of the year, adjusting their routes based on seasonal highlights, such as the vibrant wildflowers in spring or the crystal-clear mountain views in autumn.

But Madeira is more than just a natural wonder—it is a place deeply rooted in culture and history. The island's Portuguese heritage, combined with centuries of maritime exploration, has left its mark on the architecture, traditions, and cuisine. Hiking through Madeira is also a journey through time, with trails passing old stone mills, terraced vineyards, and remote villages where life continues much as it has for generations. The warmth of the Madeiran people, their hospitality, and their connection to the land add another layer of richness to every hike.

1.2 Unique Geography and Climate

Madeira's geography is a dramatic showcase of volcanic origins, rugged peaks, and lush valleys, creating an ever-changing landscape that feels almost otherworldly. The island was formed by volcanic activity millions of years ago, and while there are no active volcanoes today, the evidence of its fiery past is everywhere—from its towering basalt cliffs to its deep craters and dramatic gorges. Unlike typical volcanic islands, Madeira is incredibly green, covered in forests, terraced farmland, and high-altitude plateaus that seem to touch the sky.

One of Madeira's most striking features is its mountainous terrain, with jagged peaks that rise steeply from the ocean. The island's highest point, Pico Ruivo (1,862 meters/6,109 feet), offers hikers breathtaking panoramic views of the entire island, with rolling clouds often floating below the summit. To the south, the land slopes down to meet the coastline in a series of cliffs, some of which drop hundreds of meters straight into the Atlantic, making for some of the most dramatic coastal landscapes in the world. The Ponta de São Lourenço Peninsula, a barren and wind-swept stretch of land, contrasts sharply with the lush greenery found elsewhere, showcasing the island's diversity.

Another key feature of Madeira's landscape is its Laurisilva forest, a rare type of subtropical rainforest that once covered much of southern Europe but now remains in only a few places in the world. This UNESCO World Heritage Site is home to towering laurel trees, moss-covered rocks, and crystal-clear streams, creating a fairytale-like atmosphere. The forest plays a crucial role in Madeira's water cycle, absorbing moisture from the frequent mist and fog and feeding the island's levada system, which distributes fresh water to lower elevations.

Madeira's Year-Round Climate

Madeira's climate is as unique as its geography. Thanks to its location in the Atlantic Ocean and the influence of the Gulf Stream, the island enjoys a mild subtropical climate that makes it a year-round hiking paradise. Temperatures in coastal areas average 16–22°C (61–72°F) in winter and 22–27°C (72–81°F) in summer, while higher elevations can be cooler, sometimes even experiencing frost on the island's tallest peaks during winter.

The island's microclimates are another fascinating aspect of its environment. Madeira's north coast is generally cooler and wetter due to the prevailing trade winds, which bring moisture from the Atlantic, while the south coast tends to be drier and sunnier. This means hikers can experience lush green forests on one side of the island and semi-arid coastal landscapes on the other, sometimes in the same day.

Rain is common in the mountains, particularly in winter, but the island rarely experiences extreme weather. The warm ocean currents surrounding Madeira keep temperatures stable, ensuring that even during the hottest summer months, the climate remains pleasant for outdoor activities. However, weather conditions can change rapidly at higher elevations, so hikers should always be prepared for sudden fog, wind, or temperature drops when exploring the mountains.

Madeira's combination of dramatic volcanic landscapes, lush forests, and an ideal climate makes it one of the most attractive hiking destinations in the world. Whether climbing to a rocky summit, wandering through misty woodlands, or following a levada along a sun-drenched valley, the island's natural beauty is a constant companion, offering new surprises at every turn.

1.3 History and Cultural Significance

Beyond its natural beauty, Madeira's history and culture add another layer of depth to the hiking experience. The island's story begins long before it was settled, with ancient explorers mapping it on early navigational charts. However, it wasn't until 1419 that Portuguese sailors João Gonçalves Zarco and Tristão Vaz Teixeira officially discovered and claimed the island for Portugal. Recognising its strategic location and fertile land, the Portuguese quickly established settlements, making Madeira one of their earliest overseas territories.

A Land of Exploration and Trade

During the Age of Exploration, Madeira played a crucial role in Portugal's expansion. The island became a key stop for ships travelling between Europe, Africa, and the Americas, supplying fresh water and provisions to sailors. It also became famous for its sugarcane plantations, which brought immense wealth to the island in the 15th and 16th centuries. African slaves, brought to work on these plantations, left a lasting cultural impact on Madeira, influencing everything from music to agricultural practices.

As sugar production declined, Madeira shifted its focus to wine-making, which remains one of its most famous exports today. Madeira wine, known for its unique ageing process and rich flavours, became a favourite among European aristocrats and even American Founding Fathers—legend has it that Madeira wine was used to toast the signing of the United States Declaration of Independence.

Traditional Culture and Rural Life

Madeira's remote villages, some accessible only by footpaths for centuries, have preserved traditional ways of life. Thatched-roof houses in Santana, terraced vineyards, and old fishing harbours all tell stories of a people deeply connected to their land and the sea. The island's folklore is kept alive through music, dance, and festivals, with events like the Festa da Flor (Flower Festival) and Festa do Vinho (Wine Festival) celebrating Madeira's natural and cultural heritage.

One of the most remarkable aspects of Madeira's culture is the levada system. Built over centuries, these irrigation channels not only brought water to remote farmlands but also created an extensive network of trails used by farmers and now by hikers. Walking along these levadas is like stepping back in time, following the same paths that generations of Madeirans once used to tend their crops.

Hiking Through History

Many of Madeira's hiking trails pass through areas of historical significance. The Royal Path (Caminho Real 23), for example, was once an important trade route linking villages across the island, while trails through the Laurisilva forest lead to ancient water mills and moss-covered ruins hidden in the trees. The Vereda do Areeiro, connecting Pico do Arieiro and Pico Ruivo, follows ridges that were once used by early settlers to move between high-altitude villages.

Every step on Madeira's trails is a journey through both natural and human history.

1.4 Why Madeira is a Top Hiking Paradise in Europe

There are countless hiking destinations across Europe, from the rugged peaks of the Alps to the coastal trails of the Mediterranean. Yet, Madeira stands out as one of the continent's most unique and rewarding hiking paradises. The island offers a rare combination of dramatic landscapes, well-maintained trails, year-round accessibility, and a deep connection between nature and culture, making it a dream for hikers of all levels.

Diverse and Breathtaking Landscapes

What makes Madeira truly special is the variety of landscapes packed into such a compact island. Few places in Europe allow you to hike from towering volcanic peaks to lush rainforests, through deep gorges, and along dramatic coastal cliffs—all within a day's journey. One moment you might be ascending the rocky ridges of Pico Ruivo and Pico do Arieiro, where jagged peaks pierce through rolling clouds, and the next you're wandering through the ancient Laurisilva forest, with its moss-covered trees and hidden waterfalls.

For those drawn to the ocean, Madeira's coastal hikes, such as Ponta de São Lourenço, provide sweeping views of the Atlantic, with rugged cliffs plunging into deep blue waters. Meanwhile, the inland valleys, fed by an intricate system of waterfalls and rivers, create lush, almost tropical environments rarely found elsewhere in Europe.

The Legendary Levada Trails

One of the most defining features of Madeira's hiking scene is its levada network—a system of narrow irrigation channels built into the mountainsides to transport water from the wet northern regions to drier southern farmlands. Over the centuries, these levadas have transformed into some of the most scenic walking paths in the world.

Levada trails take hikers deep into the island's most secluded and magical landscapes, often running alongside cliffs, through hand-carved tunnels, and past cascading waterfalls. Some of the most famous include:

- Levada das 25 Fontes, leading to a hidden amphitheatre of waterfalls.
- Levada do Caldeirão Verde passes through lush forests to a spectacular emerald-green lagoon.
- Levada do Alecrim offers stunning views of high-altitude plateaus and natural pools.

These levada hikes provide an experience that is uniquely Madeiran, blending adventure, history, and the island's deep relationship with water.

Hiking in All Seasons

Unlike many European hiking destinations, which are limited to specific seasons due to snow or extreme weather, Madeira is a year-round hiking destination.

Thanks to its mild subtropical climate, the island enjoys pleasant temperatures throughout the year, with winter hikes just as enjoyable as those in summer.

Spring and autumn bring lush greenery and ideal conditions for hiking, while summer, though slightly warmer, is still comfortable due to the cooling ocean breezes. Even winter offers excellent hiking opportunities, with only the highest peaks occasionally experiencing light frost.

This lack of extreme weather means visitors don't have to worry about seasonal closures or dangerous conditions, something that makes Madeira particularly attractive for those looking for consistent hiking opportunities throughout the year.

Well-Maintained and Marked Trails

Madeira's status as a world-class hiking destination is also due to its well-developed trail infrastructure. Many of its routes are well-marked, maintained, and equipped with signposts, making navigation easier than in some other mountainous regions of Europe.

While there are still plenty of challenging and wild routes for experienced hikers, Madeira's accessibility makes it appealing to a broader range of outdoor enthusiasts. Whether you're an experienced mountaineer or someone looking for a scenic walk with breathtaking views, there's a trail for every level of experience.

A Safe and Friendly Destination

Safety is a major factor when choosing a hiking destination, and Madeira ranks among the safest places to explore in Europe. The island has low crime rates, and its well-marked trails reduce the risk of hikers getting lost. While some routes feature cliffs and require caution, the majority are safe and well-maintained, with barriers installed in more exposed areas.

Moreover, Madeira's hiking culture is welcoming, with locals often offering guidance and fellow hikers sharing advice. There is also a strong outdoor community, with guided tours and hiking groups available for those who prefer an organised experience.

A Unique Blend of Nature, Culture, and Adventure

Hiking in Madeira is more than just a physical activity—it's an immersive experience that combines natural beauty, cultural history, and adventure. The island's trails take you through places steeped in history, from old trade routes to hidden villages where traditional Madeiran life continues.

The island's festivals, traditional cuisine, and famous Madeira wine also enhance the overall experience, offering hikers a chance to unwind after a long day on the trails. Whether ending a trek with a seaside meal of grilled espada (black scabbardfish) or a glass of sweet Madeira wine, the island offers a richness that extends far beyond the trails.

Chapter 2

Planning Your Trip

2.1 Best Time to Visit Madeira for Hiking

Madeira's subtropical climate offers hikers the opportunity to explore its trails throughout the year. However, each season presents distinct conditions that can influence your hiking experience.

Spring (March to May)

Spring is arguably the perfect season to explore Madeira. During these months, the weather is typically warm and comfortable, ideal for light, summery attire, though it's wise to bring along an umbrella for sporadic rain showers. The island bursts into a kaleidoscope of vibrant blooms, making it a paradise for nature lovers.

Summer (June to August)

Summer in Madeira brings warmer temperatures, often reaching up to 27°C (81°F). The longer daylight hours provide ample time for extended hikes. However, this period coincides with the peak tourist season, leading to busier trails and higher accommodation prices. It's advisable to book accommodations well in advance to secure preferred lodging options.

Autumn (September to November)

Autumn offers mild temperatures, typically ranging from 20°C to 25°C (68°F to 77°F), and a decrease in tourist activity. This season is ideal for hikers seeking tranquillity on the trails. The landscapes remain lush, and the weather is generally stable, making it a favourable time for outdoor activities.

Winter (December to February)

Winter in Madeira is mild compared to mainland Europe, with temperatures rarely dropping below 16°C (61°F). While there is an increased chance of rainfall, many trails, especially at lower elevations, remain accessible. This off-peak season offers a more solitary hiking experience and the opportunity to explore the island without the usual crowds.

2.2 How to Get to Madeira

Madeira is accessible by air, with Cristiano Ronaldo Madeira International Airport (FNC) serving as the main gateway.

Flights to Madeira

Several airlines offer flights to Madeira from various destinations. Flight prices can vary significantly based on the departure location, time of booking, and season. For instance, round-trip flights from the United States to Madeira have been found for as low as $508. However, prices can fluctuate, so it's advisable to book in advance and monitor fares using flight comparison tools like KAYAK or Skyscanner.

Transportation on the Island

Car Rentals: Renting a car provides flexibility to explore Madeira's diverse landscapes. Several car rental companies operate at the airport and in Funchal. Prices vary depending on the vehicle type and rental duration.

Public Transportation: Madeira offers a network of public buses connecting major towns and some hiking trailheads. While affordable, the schedules may not always align with hiking plans, so it's essential to check timetables in advance.

Taxis and Ride-Sharing: Taxis are available throughout the island, and ride-sharing services operate in urban areas. For specific hikes, some taxi companies offer fixed rates to popular trailheads.

Guided Tours: For those preferring organised experiences, numerous local companies provide guided hiking tours, often including transportation, which can enhance the overall experience.

2.3 Transportation Options on the Island

Arriving in Madeira is just the first step—getting around the island is an entirely different experience. With its dramatic cliffs, deep valleys, and winding mountain roads, navigating Madeira requires some planning, especially for hikers eager to reach remote trailheads.

Unlike larger mainland destinations where trains and highways connect every major point, Madeira's terrain dictates the kind of transport options available.

For hikers looking for flexibility, renting a car is by far the best option. The island's road network is well-maintained, but drivers should be prepared for narrow, steep, and curvy roads, especially when venturing into the mountains. Automatic cars are available for rent, though they come at a higher price than manual vehicles. On average, an economy car costs between €30 and €50 per day, while an SUV, which handles mountain roads better, can range from €50 to €80 per day. Those looking for a more rugged adventure may opt for a 4x4, which can cost anywhere from €70 to €100 per day. Rental agencies can be found at Cristiano Ronaldo International Airport and throughout Funchal, though it's wise to book in advance, especially during peak hiking seasons in spring and autumn.

While a car offers freedom, Madeira's roads require confidence behind the wheel. Hairpin turns are common, and some roads have steep drops with little room for error. Fuel stations are mostly found in larger towns, with prices fluctuating between €1.70 and €2.00 per litre. Parking is generally available at major hiking points, though some of the more popular trails, like Pico do Arieiro and Rabaçal, can fill up quickly.

For those who prefer to avoid driving, Madeira's public buses provide a budget-friendly alternative, though they come with limitations. The bus network is reliable but primarily designed for locals rather than tourists, which means that while you can reach towns and some well-known hiking spots, more remote areas remain inaccessible. The main companies—Horários do Funchal, Rodoeste, SAM, and EACL—serve different regions of the island, with fares ranging from €1.50 to €5.00 depending on the route. However, bus schedules can be infrequent, particularly on weekends, so careful planning is necessary if relying on public transport.

Taxis and ride-sharing services like Uber offer a more convenient way to reach hiking trails, though they come at a higher cost. A taxi ride from Funchal to Pico do Arieiro typically costs between €25 and €35, while longer trips, such as to Rabaçal or Porto Moniz, can range from €50 to €100. Many drivers also offer private transfers to trailheads, an ideal option for groups who want a hassle-free experience without renting a car.

For those travelling in groups or looking for the most stress-free way to reach distant trails, private transfers are a practical solution. Several companies offer pre-arranged transport to hiking areas, with prices typically between €20 and €60 per trip, depending on the distance and number of passengers. Some accommodations even provide shuttle services to popular hikes, making it worth checking with hotels or lodges when booking.

2.4 Entry Requirements and Permits for Trails

Before lacing up hiking boots and setting out on Madeira's scenic trails, visitors should be aware of the island's entry requirements and hiking regulations. As an autonomous region of Portugal, Madeira follows the same entry rules as mainland Portugal, making it easy for most travellers to visit. Citizens of the European Union, Schengen Zone, the UK, the USA, Canada, and several other countries can stay visa-free for up to 90 days within 180 days. Travellers from countries requiring a visa must apply through a Portuguese consulate or embassy before their trip.

Fortunately, most of Madeira's hiking trails are free to access, with only a few exceptions requiring special permits. Many of the most famous routes, such as Pico do Arieiro to Pico Ruivo (PR1), Levada dos Balcões (PR11), and Ponta de São Lourenço (PR8), do not require any formal registration or payment. However, certain trails pass through protected areas or private lands where regulations apply. In some cases, guided hikes may involve small fees, particularly in conservation zones. The Laurisilva Forest, a UNESCO World Heritage site, has strict environmental protections, and off-trail hiking in certain areas requires prior permission from the Madeira Natural Park authorities.

While permits are rarely needed, Madeira's government enforces strict conservation rules to protect its landscapes. Hikers must stick to marked trails and avoid disturbing native vegetation, as many plant species are endemic to the island. Camping is restricted to designated areas, and fires are strictly prohibited in national parks. Additionally, drone use is regulated, and special permission is required for filming in certain protected regions.

Weather plays a major role in trail access, as conditions can change rapidly. High-altitude hikes, such as those around Pico Ruivo and Encumeada, may close temporarily due to heavy rain, landslides, or strong winds. Before heading out, checking trail conditions with the Madeira Civil Protection Authority or the local tourism board is always a good idea.

2.5 Accommodation: Hotels, Guesthouses, and Camping

Finding the right place to stay in Madeira depends on how you plan to explore the island. Whether you prefer the comfort of a hotel, the charm of a guesthouse, or the adventure of sleeping under the stars, Madeira offers a range of options that cater to different hiking styles and budgets. The choice of accommodation can also influence how easy it is to access certain trails, as some lodgings are strategically located near popular hiking routes, while others require additional transportation.

For those who want convenience and a central location, Funchal is the most popular base. As Madeira's capital, it has the widest selection of hotels, from luxury resorts to budget-friendly stays. Many hikers choose Funchal because it provides easy access to public transport, car rentals, and guided hiking tours. High-end hotels such as The Cliff Bay or Belmond Reid's Palace offer five-star comfort, with prices ranging from €200 to €500 per night. Mid-range hotels like Castanheiro Boutique Hotel or Hotel Porto Santa Maria provide a mix of affordability and quality, averaging €80 to €150 per night. Budget travellers can find hostels and guesthouses for €25 to €50 per night, with options like 29 Madeira Hostel and Santa Maria Hostel offering dormitory-style rooms.

Beyond Funchal, staying closer to the trails offers a more immersive experience. Towns such as São Vicente, Santana, and Ponta do Sol provide accommodations that bring hikers right to Madeira's stunning landscapes. In São Vicente, a gateway to some of the island's northern hikes, guesthouses like Solar da Bica offer cosy stays with mountain views for around €70 to €100 per night. Santana, known for its traditional thatched-roof houses, is ideal for those hiking Pico Ruivo or exploring the island's levadas. Here, hikers can find rural accommodations like Casa das Proteas or Quinta do Furão, with rates ranging from €80 to €150 per night.

For a more personal and local experience, guesthouses and rural lodges are a fantastic option. These family-run accommodations often provide homemade breakfasts, hiking tips, and a more relaxed atmosphere. Many guesthouses are located in traditional Madeiran villages, offering a glimpse into local life. Some, like Calhau Grande in Arco da Calheta or Casa do Ribeirinho in Porto Moniz, are designed with nature in mind, making them perfect for hikers who want quiet after a long trek.

Hikers looking for a true adventure can opt for camping. While Madeira does not have a widespread network of official campgrounds, there are designated areas where camping is permitted. The most well-known is Chão da Ribeira in Seixal, a beautiful valley surrounded by lush forest, offering a peaceful overnight stay close to nature. Another popular spot is Chão das Feiteiras, near Pico do Arieiro, which provides a cooler mountain atmosphere. Camping is free in designated areas, but a permit must be obtained from the Instituto das Florestas e Conservação da Natureza (IFCN). Wild camping is not generally allowed, except in a few remote regions with prior authorisation.

For those who enjoy being in the mountains but prefer more comfort, mountain huts and eco-lodges provide a middle ground between camping and hotels. The Casa de Abrigo do Pico Ruivo, located near Madeira's highest peak, offers basic shelter for hikers who want to experience sunrise from the summit. Spaces are limited, and reservations are required in advance. Other eco-lodges, such as Cabanas São Jorge Village, offer wooden cabins surrounded by nature, blending comfort with a wilderness experience.

Chapter 3

Budgeting for Your Hiking Adventure

3.1 Cost of Accommodation and Food

Planning a hiking trip to Madeira isn't just about mapping out trails and packing the right gear—it also means budgeting for essentials like accommodation and food. The good news is that Madeira offers a variety of lodging and dining options, making it possible to plan a trip that suits different budgets, whether you're a backpacker seeking affordable stays or a traveler looking for a bit of comfort after long hikes.

Accommodation Costs

Madeira's accommodation scene is diverse, ranging from budget-friendly hostels to luxurious resorts overlooking the Atlantic. Prices fluctuate based on the season, location, and level of comfort.

Budget Travelers ($15–$40 per night): Hostels and guesthouses in Funchal or smaller villages provide shared dormitories or basic private rooms. Camping is another budget-friendly option, with some official campsites charging small fees, while wild camping requires permission in designated areas.

Mid-Range Hotels and Guesthouses ($50–$120 per night): Cosy guesthouses, traditional quintas (country estates), and mid-range hotels offer comfortable stays with scenic views. These are excellent choices for those wanting a balance between affordability and convenience.

Luxury Resorts and Boutique Hotels ($150–$500+ per night): For travelers looking for high-end experiences, Madeira boasts stunning cliffside resorts, spa hotels, and boutique accommodations. These often include amenities like infinity pools, guided hikes, and fine dining.

Peak hiking seasons—spring (March to May) and autumn (September to November)—often see higher rates, so booking early can help secure better deals.

Food Costs

Dining in Madeira can be surprisingly affordable, especially if you enjoy local flavours. Traditional Madeiran cuisine is rich in fresh seafood, tropical fruits, and hearty stews. While restaurants in Funchal's touristy areas tend to be pricier, venturing into smaller towns or local eateries (tascas) provides excellent meals at a fraction of the cost.

Street Food & Bakeries ($3–$8 per meal): A simple yet delicious meal can be found in pastelarias (bakeries) serving fresh pão de deus (coconut bread) or bolo do caco (Madeiran flatbread with garlic butter). You'll also find cheap and tasty espetadas (grilled meat skewers) at roadside stalls.

Casual Restaurants & Local Taverns ($10–$20 per meal): Many local restaurants serve espetada, scabbardfish with banana, or a hearty bowl of milho frito (fried cornmeal cubes) at reasonable prices. Daily menus (pratos do dia) are an excellent way to enjoy local dishes without spending too much.

Fine Dining ($40–$100+ per meal): Upscale restaurants specialising in seafood and gourmet Madeiran dishes provide a high-end experience. These often include wine pairings with local Madeira wine.

For budget-conscious hikers, self-catering is an option. Local markets offer fresh produce, cheese, and bread, making it easy to prepare your own meals or pack trail snacks.

3.2 Transportation Expenses:

Getting to Madeira and moving around the island efficiently plays a key role in the overall cost of your trip. Transportation expenses vary depending on how you choose to arrive, travel between towns, and explore hiking trails.

Flights to Madeira

Madeira's main gateway is Cristiano Ronaldo International Airport (FNC), located near Funchal. The cost of flights depends on your departure city, season, and airline.

From Europe: Budget airlines like Ryanair, easyJet, and TAP Air Portugal frequently offer flights from major European cities. Round-trip fares range from $100–$400, with lower prices found outside peak seasons.

From North America: There are no direct flights from the U.S. or Canada, but travelers typically connect via Lisbon or Porto. Round-trip fares from New York or Toronto range between $600–$1,200, depending on the time of year.

From Other Regions: If coming from Asia, Australia, or South America, expect multiple layovers, with average fares exceeding $1,000.

Booking flights early—especially for peak hiking months—helps secure better prices.

Local Transportation on Madeira

Once on the island, hikers have multiple ways to get around:

Public Buses ($2–$6 per ride): Buses are the most economical option, covering key towns and popular hiking areas. SAM, Rodoeste, and Horários do Funchal operate routes, but schedules can be limited in remote areas.

Taxis & Ride-Sharing ($15–$40 per trip): Taxis are common but can be expensive for long distances. Some areas also have Bolt, a cheaper ride-hailing alternative.

Car Rentals ($30–$80 per day): Renting a car provides flexibility, especially for accessing trailheads early in the morning. However, Madeira's steep roads require confident driving.

Private Transfers & Tour Shuttles ($20–$100 per ride): Many tour companies offer transfers to hiking spots like Pico do Arieiro and Levada das 25 Fontes, useful for one-way hikes where public transport isn't an option.

Additional Transportation Costs

Cable Cars & Funiculars ($5–$15 per ride): Some remote areas, like Fajã dos Padres or Achadas da Cruz, require cable car access.

Ferries to Porto Santo ($40–$80 round-trip): If planning a side trip to Porto Santo, consider ferry expenses.

3.3 Trail Costs:

Hiking in Madeira is one of the most accessible outdoor activities, with many trails open to the public at no cost. The island's network of levadas and mountain paths offers endless opportunities to explore lush forests, breathtaking cliffs, and rugged peaks without needing to pay entry fees. However, while most hikes are free, some require additional costs depending on the location, difficulty level, and whether a hiker chooses to go independently or with a guide.

For solo hikers, permits are generally not required for most trails, but there are exceptions. Certain protected areas, such as parts of the Laurisilva Forest, may require special permissions for conservation purposes, though these are rarely enforced for casual visitors. Some levada walks pass through private land, and while access is usually granted freely, there are rare cases where small fees may apply. One of the most notable expenses comes from shuttle services, such as those at Rabaçal, where a return ride to the start of the famous Levada das 25 Fontes costs around €5 per person—a small price to pay to avoid a steep uphill walk after a long trek.

For those who prefer a structured experience, guided hikes are widely available, providing expert knowledge about the island's landscapes, flora, fauna, and history. Prices for guided hikes vary depending on the route, group size, and level of exclusivity. Standard group tours typically cost between €25 and €50 per person, covering transport from Funchal and surrounding areas, professional guidance, and sometimes small refreshments. Private guided hikes, which allow for more flexibility and tailored experiences, range from €80 to €150, with prices increasing for specialized tours such as photography excursions or bird-watching treks. Some companies even offer luxury hiking experiences that include gourmet meals, premium transport, or overnight stays in remote mountain lodges.

For multi-day hikes or travelers who don't want to carry heavy equipment from home, gear rental is a practical option. Basic hiking poles can be rented for around €5 per day, while headlamps—essential for tunnel walks like Levada do Caldeirão Verde—cost between €3 and €6 per day. Backpack rentals vary depending on size, starting at €10 per day, while full camping kits, including tents and sleeping bags, range from €20 to €40 per day. Outdoor stores in Funchal and key hiking areas like Santana or Porto Moniz provide easy access to these rentals, ensuring that visitors can hike comfortably without overpacking.

While Madeira's trails are generally accessible at little to no cost, hikers should always budget for optional expenses such as transportation, gear, or professional guidance. Whether choosing to hike independently or with a guide, knowing the potential costs in advance allows visitors to plan efficiently, ensuring a smooth and enjoyable hiking experience.

3.4 Budgeting Tips for Different Traveler Types

Madeira caters to every kind of traveler, from budget backpackers looking to experience its natural beauty affordably to luxury seekers wanting a high-end adventure. Understanding how to allocate funds efficiently can help visitors make the most of their trip without unexpected expenses.

For budget travelers, it is entirely possible to hike Madeira's trails while spending as little as €30 to €60 per day. Affordable hostels in Funchal and smaller towns cost around €20 to €35 per night, while camping in designated areas is sometimes free or costs no more than

€5 to €10 per night. Supermarkets such as Pingo Doce and Continente offer fresh local produce and budget-friendly meals, with sandwiches and pastries available for as little as €2 to €5. Public buses, though less frequent than private transport, provide access to major hiking areas at fares between €1.50 and €5, making them an excellent option for those travelling light. Additionally, many of the island's best trails—including Pico Ruivo, Levada do Alecrim, and Vereda dos Balcões—are completely free to access, making it easy to enjoy world-class hiking without spending extra.

For those travelling on a mid-range budget, spending typically falls between €70 and €150 per day. This allows for more comfortable accommodations in guesthouses or mid-range hotels, which range from €50 to €100 per night, depending on location and season. Renting a car, one of the best ways to explore Madeira, costs around €30 to €50 per day, though prices can rise during peak seasons. Dining at local restaurants such as traditional "espetada" steakhouses or seafood taverns typically costs between €10 and €20 per meal, allowing travelers to experience Madeiran cuisine without overspending. Mid-range travelers may also choose to join a few guided hikes, typically costing €25 to €50 per person, to gain deeper insights into the island's history and ecology while still enjoying plenty of independent exploration.

For those seeking a luxury experience, Madeira offers premium options that elevate the hiking journey. With a budget of €200 or more per day, travellers can enjoy stays in five-star hotels such as Belmond Reid's Palace or

Savoy Palace, where rooms start at €250 per night. High-end dining at Michelin-starred restaurants like William or Il Gallo d'Oro offers exquisite local flavours, with tasting menus starting at €80 to €150 per person. Private hiking guides, offering exclusive access to lesser-known trails, cost around €100 to €200 per hike, and for those looking to explore Madeira in the most extravagant way possible, helicopter tours over the island's peaks start at €250 per person. Chauffeur-driven tours, yacht rentals, and spa experiences can all be incorporated into a luxury hiking itinerary, ensuring an unforgettable experience.

Regardless of budget, careful planning allows visitors to enjoy Madeira to the fullest. Bookings help secure lower accommodation and transport costs, while travelling during the shoulder seasons—spring and autumn—provides ideal weather conditions without peak-season pricing. Packing appropriately can also help reduce unnecessary expenses, as buying gear on the island can be costly for those unprepared.

Chapter 4

Essential Gear and Packing Guide

Hiking in Madeira is an experience unlike any other, with trails that wind through ancient laurel forests, ascend rugged volcanic peaks, and follow the famous levadas—the island's historic irrigation channels. But with such breathtaking scenery comes the need for careful preparation. Madeira's terrain is diverse, ranging from well-maintained paths to steep, rocky ascents, while its climate is just as varied, with rapidly shifting weather conditions influenced by the island's altitude and Atlantic location. Packing the right gear ensures not only comfort but also safety, allowing hikers to fully embrace the adventure without unnecessary setbacks.

4.1 Clothing and Footwear for Madeira's Terrain

The key to dressing for Madeira's hikes is adaptability. The island's microclimates mean that a warm, sunny morning along the coastline can quickly turn into a misty, cool afternoon in the mountains. The higher-altitude trails, particularly those around Pico Ruivo (1,862 m) and Pico do Arieiro (1,818 m), often experience strong winds and sudden temperature drops, while the laurel forests of Fanal and Rabaçal can be damp and cool even when lower elevations remain dry.

For this reason, layering is the best approach. A moisture-wicking base layer helps regulate body temperature, keeping sweat away from the skin and preventing chills. A light fleece or insulated mid-layer provides warmth for early mornings and higher elevations. The outer layer should always be a waterproof and windproof jacket, as rain showers and strong Atlantic gusts are common, especially in exposed areas. Even in the dry season, it's not unusual for mist and drizzle to roll in unexpectedly, particularly in the mountains.

Footwear is equally important, as Madeira's trails vary significantly in difficulty. Many of the levada walks, such as Levada das 25 Fontes or Levada do Caldeirão Verde, feature relatively flat paths where lightweight hiking shoes with good grip are sufficient. However, more challenging routes, like the Vereda da Encumeada or the Vereda do Larano coastal trail, require sturdy hiking boots with ankle support to handle steep inclines, rocky surfaces, and potentially slippery sections. Waterproof footwear is highly recommended, as many trails pass through damp forests or involve crossing small streams. Moisture-wicking socks help prevent blisters, while gaiters can keep dirt and water out of boots on muddier hikes.

Accessories like a wide-brimmed hat or a cap with a neck cover are essential for sun protection on exposed trails.

Sunglasses with UV protection help reduce glare, particularly on the white volcanic rock of high-altitude routes. Hiking poles are useful on steep descents, reducing strain on the knees, especially on long trails like PR1 Vereda do Areeiro.

4.2 Navigation Tools:

Despite being well-marked, Madeira's trails can be challenging to navigate due to dense vegetation, foggy conditions, and sudden weather changes that obscure visibility. While official trail signs are placed at major intersections, it's always wise to have additional navigation tools to avoid getting lost, especially on lesser-known routes.

Carrying a physical map is a crucial backup, particularly in remote areas where mobile signals can be unreliable. The Madeira Walks & Trails official map, available at tourist offices in Funchal and other major towns, provides detailed information on routes, difficulty levels, and elevation changes.

For digital navigation, GPS devices or smartwatches with built-in maps offer real-time tracking and elevation profiles, ensuring hikers stay on course. Several mobile apps also help with navigation and trip planning. AllTrails provides user reviews, trail difficulty ratings, and downloadable offline maps. Maps.me is another useful option for offline navigation, while Komoot and

Wikiloc offer community-sourced GPS tracks that guide hikers along established routes.

Given the length of many hikes, a portable power bank is a must-have to keep phones and GPS devices charged throughout the day. Some trails, particularly in the Laurisilva forest, have dense tree cover that drains batteries faster due to constant signal searching.

4.3 Food and Water Considerations for Hikers

When hiking in Madeira, staying properly fueled and hydrated is key to enjoying the trails and ensuring your safety, especially considering the challenging terrain and varying climates. While the island offers an abundance of natural beauty, the resources for hikers are somewhat limited in remote areas, so preparation is essential.

Water is the most important element to carry on any hike, especially since many trails traverse mountainous and forested areas where access to fresh water is scarce. While some of the more popular levada trails might have water sources along the way, relying solely on these can be risky, as some of the streams may not always be safe for drinking. It's always best to carry at least 1.5 to 2 litres of water per person, particularly on longer or higher-altitude hikes. For high-altitude trails like Pico do Arieiro to Pico Ruivo, where the air is thinner and dehydration can occur more quickly, it's even more important to stay hydrated. A hydration pack or water bottles are essential for ensuring you can sip water consistently without needing to stop and unpack. A water filter or purification tablets are also useful if you plan on drinking from streams or water sources along the trail, but always ensure you are familiar with proper usage and safety precautions.

Food is just as important. Long hikes on Madeira's challenging terrain demand sustained energy, so it's crucial to pack a variety of high-energy snacks that are easy to carry and won't spoil. Opt for trail mix with a mix of nuts, seeds, and dried fruit for quick energy. Granola bars, energy gels, and protein bars are also excellent choices, offering quick and easy calories without weighing you down. For a more substantial meal, consider packing sandwiches or wraps filled with lean protein, cheese, and vegetables, ensuring they'll last the entire day. Fresh fruit like apples and bananas can provide a good natural energy boost, but should be consumed early in the hike to avoid them getting squished in your bag.

If you are hiking on longer or more remote trails where there may be no access to food supplies, consider packing an emergency ration pack or a small cooking setup for hot meals. While not necessary for short hikes, a small stove and some freeze-dried meals can make for a comforting break, particularly on multi-day hikes.

Energy drinks and electrolyte tablets are also a good idea to replace the minerals lost through sweat, especially on hot days. On trails with significant elevation gain, such as those around Pico Ruivo, your body will burn through energy reserves quickly, so having a mix of quick carbs and longer-lasting foods is key.

4.4 Packing List for Different Seasons

Packing for hiking in Madeira requires adaptability, as the island's diverse geography and unique climate can shift dramatically from one area to the next, and from one season to another. Here's a breakdown of what to pack for different times of the year to ensure you're prepared no matter the conditions.

Spring and Summer (March to August)

During the warmer months, Madeira's lower altitudes enjoy mild temperatures, and the higher elevations are often crisp with cooler evenings. Here's what you'll need:

Clothing: Lightweight, moisture-wicking base layers are essential to stay cool during warmer days. A long-sleeve shirt made from breathable material protects against sun exposure, while lightweight pants or shorts give you comfort without compromising on flexibility. For sun protection, carry a hat with a wide brim to shield your face and neck.

Outerwear: A light rain jacket or windbreaker is important in case of sudden showers, which can occur unexpectedly even in summer.

Footwear: Opt for breathable, lightweight hiking shoes for the lower-altitude trails. However, if you're tackling higher, more rugged terrain, sturdy, waterproof hiking boots are recommended for rocky or uneven paths.

Accessories: Sunglasses are essential to protect your eyes from UV rays. Sunscreen should be applied regularly, and a small daypack will help carry your water, food, and essentials.

Autumn (September to November)

Autumn brings cooler temperatures, particularly at higher elevations, and more rainfall. The island's forests and volcanic landscapes will be lush with colour, but the trails can get slippery after rain. Here's what to pack:

Clothing: Layering becomes crucial as temperatures fluctuate throughout the day. A long-sleeve moisture-wicking shirt and warm fleece jacket are ideal for cooler mornings and evenings. You'll need water-resistant pants to prevent dampness from the trails.

Outerwear: A heavier waterproof and windproof jacket is essential, as autumn often sees frequent rainfall and wind gusts, especially in the mountains.

Footwear: Opt for waterproof hiking boots to navigate wet, muddy trails. Ensure the boots are sturdy and provide ankle support for slippery paths.

Accessories: Carry a poncho for extra protection in heavy rain, along with extra socks to prevent blisters. A small first-aid kit for blister care is a good idea for this season.

Winter (December to February)

Winter in Madeira brings much cooler temperatures, and at higher altitudes, it can even snow. While coastal areas remain mild, the mountains will be cold, and you should expect fog, wind, and rain. Here's what you'll need to pack for winter hiking:

Clothing: Thermal base layers are essential to keep warm, particularly in the mountains. Pair them with insulated jackets for additional warmth, and bring thermal socks for your feet. Waterproof gloves and a hat are important, as temperatures can drop significantly in the mountains, especially at night.

Outerwear: You'll need a heavier waterproof jacket to protect against both rain and wind. A waterproof, insulated vest might also come in handy for added warmth in windy areas.

Footwear: Ensure you have sturdy, waterproof boots that offer insulation and grip, as snowy or icy conditions may be present at higher elevations.

Accessories: Headlamps or flashlights become crucial if you plan on long hikes or early starts, as daylight hours are shorter. A thermal flask with hot drinks can be a welcome boost during cold-weather hikes.

Chapter 5

Top Hiking Trails in Madeira

5.1 Levada do Caldeirão Verde – Lush Forests and Waterfalls

The Levada do Caldeirão Verde is one of Madeira's most enchanting hikes, offering a journey through dense laurel forests, moss-covered cliffs, and a series of cascading waterfalls that seem untouched by time. This trail, located in the Queimadas Forest Park in Santana, follows an ancient levada (irrigation channel) originally built in the 18th century to carry water from the mountains to agricultural lands. Today, it serves as a breathtaking hiking route, drawing visitors eager to explore Madeira's lush interior.

The hike begins at the Queimadas Forestry Park, where a charming thatched-roof house sits like something out of a fairytale, setting the tone for the adventure ahead. From here, the path follows the levada, winding through a landscape dominated by Madeira's Laurisilva forest, a UNESCO World Heritage Site. The thick canopy overhead provides shade, while ferns and wildflowers thrive along the damp trail. As hikers progress, they pass through a series of narrow tunnels carved into the mountainside. These tunnels, remnants of the island's old water management system, require a flashlight and a bit of caution, but they add to the sense of exploration.

The real highlight of the trek is Caldeirão Verde, a striking emerald-green lagoon fed by a towering 100-meter waterfall. The sight of water plunging from the cliffs above into the tranquil pool below is nothing short of mesmerizing. Many hikers pause here for a break, dipping their hands into the cool water or enjoying a packed lunch surrounded by nature's finest scenery. The return journey retraces the same path, offering new perspectives of the towering valleys and distant ocean views visible through breaks in the forest.

Covering about 13 kilometres (8 miles) round trip, the Levada do Caldeirão Verde is a moderately challenging hike, taking around 4 to 5 hours to complete. The path is mostly flat but includes some narrow sections with sheer drop-offs, where protective railings help ensure safety. Given the humid conditions, sturdy hiking shoes with good grip are recommended, and a rain jacket is advisable as the forest often experiences light mist or drizzle. This levada walk is a must-do for those looking to immerse themselves in Madeira's green heart.

5.2 Levada das 25 Fontes – Iconic Waterfall Hike

Tucked within the lush landscapes of Rabaçal, the Levada das 25 Fontes is one of Madeira's most famous and rewarding hikes, known for its series of natural springs and an unforgettable waterfall finale. This scenic trail follows an ancient levada system, meandering through dense forests, mossy ravines, and striking volcanic rock formations, making it a dream for nature lovers. The adventure begins at the Rabaçal Forestry House, where hikers descend into the valley along a paved road. The first stretch of the trail runs alongside the Levada do Risco, offering a preview of what's to come with the impressive Risco Waterfall, which spills over a towering basalt wall in a dramatic curtain of water. From here, the trail splits, leading deeper into the forest toward the main highlight—the 25 Fontes (25 Springs).

As the name suggests, the 25 Fontes is a natural amphitheatre where numerous small springs trickle down a moss-covered cliff into a crystal-clear lagoon. The scene is magical, with the gentle sound of running water and birdsong filling the air. Many hikers pause here to soak in the beauty, snap photos, or even dip their feet into the cool water. The round-trip distance is approximately 11 kilometres (6.8 miles) and takes around 4 to 5 hours to complete. The trail includes some steep inclines and uneven stone steps, making sturdy hiking boots essential. Given its popularity, it's best to start early in the morning to avoid crowds, especially during peak hiking months.

5.3 Levada do Rei – Walk Through Madeira's Laurisilva Forest

For those seeking a peaceful yet visually stunning hike, Levada do Rei offers an incredible journey through

Madeira's ancient Laurisilva forest, a UNESCO World Heritage Site. This trail, which translates to the "King's Levada," follows a gentle path through one of the island's most well-preserved natural landscapes, providing a glimpse into what Madeira looked like long before human settlement. The trail begins near São Jorge, on the north side of the island, where the levada winds through rolling green hills before plunging into a dense, misty forest. Towering laurel, mahogany, and heather trees create a lush canopy overhead, while the ground is covered in mosses, ferns, and wildflowers. The air is crisp, filled with the scent of damp earth and fresh vegetation, making it a refreshing escape from Madeira's coastal heat.

As hikers follow the levada deeper into the forest, they pass through small waterfalls trickling down rock faces, feeding into the levada's clear waters. One of the most striking aspects of this hike is the contrast between the open valley views and the enclosed, almost mystical atmosphere of the Laurisilva forest. The path is relatively easy, making it accessible to hikers of all experience levels, though occasional narrow sections require careful footing.

The final stretch of the trail leads to the Ribeiro Bonito, a secluded gorge where the levada disappears into a curtain of thick vegetation. This spot, with its small waterfalls and towering green walls, feels almost untouched by time. Many hikers choose to rest here, listening to the soothing sounds of running water and birdsong before retracing their steps back to the trailhead.

At 10 kilometres (6.2 miles) round-trip, Levada do Rei takes around 3 to 4 hours to complete. The trail is mostly flat, making it suitable for families and beginner hikers, though waterproof shoes are recommended due to the moist conditions. This hike is a perfect introduction to Madeira's Laurisilva forest, offering a serene and immersive nature experience unlike any other.

5.4 Levada do Alecrim – Tranquil Waterfall and Lagoon

Tucked away in the highlands of Rabaçal, the Levada do Alecrim is one of Madeira's most peaceful and rewarding hikes, leading to a hidden waterfall and a tranquil lagoon. Unlike some of the island's more challenging hikes, this levada walk offers a relaxed pace with breathtaking scenery, making it a favorite for those looking to enjoy nature without an intense climb. The trail starts at an altitude of around 1,300 meters, offering sweeping views of the Paul da Serra plateau, a vast expanse of rolling hills and open skies. From the very beginning, the levada follows a clear, gently flowing stream, with wildflowers and shrubs lining the path. The higher altitude means the air is cooler, providing a refreshing contrast to the more humid levada walks found in lower regions.

As hikers progress, they encounter small waterfalls and pools where the water glistens under the sunlight. The real highlight, however, comes at the end of the trail—Lagoa Dona Beja, a stunning natural lagoon fed by a cascading waterfall. The water, clear and cool, invites visitors to pause, take in the surroundings, and even dip their feet into the shallow pools. Unlike some of the busier levada hikes, Levada do Alecrim remains relatively quiet, adding to its charm as a place of relaxation and solitude. The trail is approximately 7 kilometres (4.3 miles) round-trip and takes about 2 to 3 hours to complete. The gentle incline and well-maintained path make it an ideal choice for casual hikers, though good walking shoes are recommended to navigate occasional rocky sections. Since this area is more exposed, sun protection is also advisable, especially during midday hikes.

5.5 Pico Ruivo – The Highest Peak of Madeira

The journey to Pico Ruivo, Madeira's highest peak at 1,862 meters, is nothing short of breathtaking. Standing at the summit, with an endless sea of clouds rolling below and the jagged peaks of the island stretching into the distance, it feels as if you've reached the very top of the world. The crisp mountain air carries the scent of wildflowers and damp earth, a reminder of the island's rich volcanic origins. There are several ways to reach Pico Ruivo, each offering a unique experience. The most accessible route begins at Achada do Teixeira, where a 2.8-kilometre trail gently ascends toward the summit. This path is ideal for those looking for a rewarding hike without the strenuous challenge of steep climbs. Along the way, the trail cuts through sections of ancient Laurisilva forest, where the twisted branches of moss-covered trees create a mystical atmosphere. As you climb higher, the landscape opens up to reveal sweeping views of the valleys below, with occasional glimpses of the ocean shimmering in the distance.

For those seeking a more demanding adventure, the route from Encumeada offers a full-day trek through some of Madeira's most rugged mountain terrain. This trail winds through deep ravines, past sheer rock faces, and along ridgelines that drop dramatically into the valleys below. The changing scenery—from dense forest to exposed volcanic rock—makes every step of the journey a discovery. Reaching the summit of Pico Ruivo is a triumphant moment, and whether you arrive at sunrise, when the first light paints the peaks in soft hues of gold, or at sunset, when the sky turns a deep shade of crimson, the view is nothing short of unforgettable.

5.6 Pico do Arieiro to Pico Ruivo – The Ultimate Mountain Traverse

Few trails in Madeira match the dramatic beauty and exhilarating challenge of the Pico do Arieiro to Pico Ruivo hike. This 11-kilometre route connects two of the island's most iconic peaks, winding through sheer cliffs, narrow mountain ridges, and hidden tunnels carved into the rock. It's a trail that demands strength and determination, but for those who take on the challenge, it offers some of the most stunning views in all of Madeira.

The adventure begins at Pico do Arieiro, where the morning sun casts long shadows across the rugged peaks, and clouds swirl around the lower valleys. Standing at the viewpoint, the entire island unfolds beneath you, an unbroken expanse of mountains stretching toward the Atlantic. From here, the descent into the mountains begins, with steep steps leading down toward a series of ridges that seem to defy gravity. At times, the trail is little more than a narrow path carved into the mountainside, with sheer drop-offs plunging into the valleys below. The famous Stairway to Heaven, a dramatic set of stairs leading up a knife-edge ridge, is both thrilling and daunting—each step bringing you closer to the heart of Madeira's mountainous wilderness.

As the trail continues, it weaves through tunnels hewn from solid rock, their cool, damp interiors offering a brief respite from the sun. Emerging on the other side, the final ascent to Pico Ruivo begins, the landscape shifting once again as the jagged volcanic rock gives way to softer slopes covered in alpine vegetation. The last stretch is a steady climb, the anticipation growing with every step. And then, at the summit, the reward—an awe-inspiring panorama of Madeira's peaks, valleys, and coastline, stretching as far as the eye can see.

5.7 Vereda da Ponta de São Lourenço – Dramatic Coastal Hike

The Vereda da Ponta de São Lourenço is unlike any other hike on Madeira. This trail, stretching across the island's easternmost peninsula, trades the lush greenery of the Laurisilva forests for a rugged, almost otherworldly landscape shaped by wind and waves. Here, the cliffs are jagged, the vegetation sparse, and the ocean stretches endlessly in both directions, its deep blue contrasting with the burnt-red and ochre hues of the volcanic rock.

The hike begins at Baía d'Abra, where the trail immediately introduces you to the raw beauty of the peninsula. With no trees to offer shade, the sun beats down on the open landscape, while the constant ocean breeze carries the scent of salt and wildflowers clinging to the rocky slopes. The path winds along dramatic sea cliffs, offering breathtaking views at every turn. On one side, the Atlantic crashes against towering rock faces, sending white spray into the air. On the other hand, sheltered coves reveal calm, turquoise waters where seabirds nest on the rocky outcrops.

As you move deeper into the hike, the landscape becomes even more striking. The contrast between the northern and southern coastlines of the peninsula is stark—one side battered by the rough Atlantic waves, the other calmer and more serene. The trail is well-marked but undulating, with a series of climbs and descents that add to the challenge. Eventually, you reach Pico do Furado, the highest point of the peninsula, where the panoramic view is nothing short of breathtaking. On clear days, you can see the nearby Desertas Islands, their rocky silhouettes rising from the ocean, and even the distant Porto Santo on the far horizon.

For those wanting to cool off, a short detour leads to Cais do Sardinha, a small, secluded bay with clear waters perfect for a refreshing swim. The final stretch of the trail takes you toward the São Lourenço viewpoint, where the peninsula dramatically narrows before disappearing into the sea. The return journey follows the same path, offering another chance to take in the wild beauty of Madeira's most dramatic coastal hike.

5.8 Encumeada Pass – Exploring Madeira's Mountainous Heart

At the very heart of Madeira's mountainous interior lies Encumeada Pass, a place where misty valleys, ancient forests, and towering peaks converge to create one of the island's most rewarding hiking experiences. Nestled between the central mountain range, this region offers a deep connection to Madeira's rugged landscape, where hikers can traverse high-altitude ridges and descend into dense woodlands in a single journey.

The trail begins at Boca da Encumeada, a scenic mountain pass that serves as a gateway to both the northern and southern sides of the island. The first section of the hike follows a steady incline, leading into the heart of Madeira's Laurisilva forest, a UNESCO World Heritage Site. Here, the air is thick with the earthy scent of damp moss, and the sunlight filters through a canopy of ancient trees, casting patterns of light and shadow on the path below. The sound of trickling water is ever-present, as natural springs and small waterfalls emerge from the mountainside, feeding the levadas that crisscross the landscape. As the trail climbs higher, the vegetation thins, giving way to breathtaking ridgeline views. Encumeada is one of the few places on the island where you can see both the northern and southern coastlines at once, a sight made even more dramatic when the morning mist rolls through the valleys, creating a dreamlike atmosphere. The peaks of Pico Grande, Pico do Jorge, and Pico Ruivo stand majestically in the distance, their rocky faces shifting in color as the sun moves overhead.

For those seeking a challenge, an extended hike from Encumeada leads toward Pico Ruivo, traversing rugged mountain paths with sections of steep inclines and dramatic drop-offs. This route requires stamina but rewards hikers with some of the most spectacular landscapes Madeira has to offer. Along the way, small wooden shelters provide resting spots, where you can pause to take in the panoramic views and listen to the occasional call of a buzzard soaring overhead. The descent back to Encumeada follows a different route, passing through hidden valleys and remote sections of forest where the only sounds are the rustling leaves and distant echoes of water cascading down the rocks.

5.9 Boca do Risco – Cliffside Ocean Views

Boca do Risco is a breathtaking coastal hike that combines adventure with spectacular ocean views. This trail follows the edge of Madeira's dramatic northern cliffs, where steep, green slopes plunge into the Atlantic below. Unlike the levadas, which often meander through forests, this hike offers a continuous view of the endless blue sea, making it one of the best routes for coastal scenery. The most common way to access Boca do Risco is from the town of Machico, following the Vereda da Boca do Risco trail. The path ascends gently at first, cutting through eucalyptus forests before emerging onto an exposed ridgeline with views stretching toward the distant Ponta de São Lourenço. As hikers reach the Boca do Risco viewpoint, they are greeted by a sweeping panorama of Madeira's untamed coastline, with waves crashing far below.

For those seeking more adventure, the trail can be extended westward toward Porto da Cruz, creating a longer, more demanding coastal trek. However, this section features narrow paths along cliffs, requiring caution, especially on windy days. The best time for this hike is during the dry season (April to October), when visibility is best, and the ground is more stable.

5.10 Porto Moniz Coastal Trails – Lava Pools and Rugged Cliffs

The Porto Moniz coastal trails offer a unique hiking experience in Madeira's northwestern corner, where volcanic rock formations meet the relentless force of the Atlantic. Porto Moniz is famous for its natural lava pools, but beyond the popular swimming areas lies a network of lesser-explored hiking paths that reveal the wild beauty of the island's coastline.

One of the most stunning routes in this area is the trail leading from Porto Moniz to Achadas da Cruz, a remote and scenic journey along rugged cliffs. The path begins near the lava pools, winding upward to reveal towering basalt formations, sea caves, and black sand beaches hidden between rocky outcrops. The landscape here feels almost prehistoric, shaped by ancient volcanic activity and the powerful Atlantic tides.

For a shorter but equally rewarding hike, the Levada da Ribeira da Janela offers a different perspective. This levada trail follows a narrow water channel inland, leading hikers through dense forests and misty valleys before opening up to sweeping views of the coast. It's a fantastic option for those who want to combine coastal scenery with Madeira's rich biodiversity.

Since this area is more exposed to the elements, hikers should check weather conditions before setting out. Winter storms can bring strong waves and high winds, making some trails dangerous or impassable.

5.11 Paul da Serra – Madeira's High Plateau Hikes

Paul da Serra is a vast, high-altitude plateau that feels like a world apart from the cliffs and lush valleys below. Unlike the dense forests of the levada trails, this area features open landscapes, rolling hills, and windswept fields, offering a different kind of hiking experience. Situated at an altitude of 1,400–1,600 meters, it is the flattest region in Madeira, providing wide panoramic views over the mountains and coast. Hiking in Paul da Serra offers an opportunity to explore some of Madeira's most remote and peaceful trails. The Vereda do Fanal is a standout route, leading to the enchanting Fanal Forest, a UNESCO-listed Laurisilva woodland where ancient, moss-covered trees create a surreal, misty atmosphere. This trail is particularly beautiful in the morning, when low-hanging fog drifts through the gnarled trees, creating an almost dreamlike setting.

Another excellent option is the Rabaçal and 25 Fontes route, which descends from the plateau into a series of lush valleys and waterfalls. While this trail is more well-known, it starts at Paul da Serra, making it a convenient hike for those exploring the plateau. Due to its altitude, Paul da Serra can experience rapid weather changes. Mornings are often cool and misty, while afternoons can be sunny and warm. Hikers should be prepared for sudden shifts in temperature and bring windproof and waterproof layers.

Chapter 6

Seasonal Hiking and Weather Considerations

Madeira's mild, subtropical climate makes it a year-round hiking destination, but each season brings different conditions that can dramatically affect the experience on the trails. The island's mountainous terrain creates microclimates, meaning that while the coastline may be sunny and warm, the peaks can be shrouded in mist or even frost. Understanding the best times to hike based on weather, visibility, and natural beauty is key to planning an enjoyable and safe adventure.

6.1 Best Months for Clear Views on Peaks

For those seeking crystal-clear views from Madeira's highest peaks, the best time to hike is during the late spring, summer, and early autumn months—specifically from May to October. During this period, the island experiences the least amount of rainfall, and weather conditions are generally more stable, making it easier to enjoy panoramic vistas from summits like Pico Ruivo (1,862m) and Pico do Arieiro (1,818m).

The summer months of July and August offer the most reliable weather, with minimal cloud cover at higher elevations. However, these months can also be the warmest, particularly on exposed ridge trails such as Vereda do Pico Ruivo or the Pico do Arieiro to Pico Ruivo traverse, where shade is scarce. Morning hikes are recommended during this time to avoid peak daytime heat.

September and October are also excellent months for clear views, as the weather remains dry, but the summer crowds begin to thin. Autumn often brings more dramatic sunrises and sunsets, with warm golden hues lighting up the rugged peaks.

Winter (November to March) brings higher chances of cloud cover and rain, especially in Madeira's mountains. The peaks can sometimes be hidden in thick fog, limiting visibility. However, there are occasional clear days when the air is crisp, and the views stretch for miles. Checking real-time weather forecasts before setting out is essential, as conditions can change rapidly at high altitudes.

Tip for Clear Views:

- Start hikes early in the morning. Cloud cover tends to develop as the day progresses, particularly in the mountains.
- Check the webcams at Pico Ruivo and Pico do Arieiro before heading out to see current conditions.
- Avoid stormy days, as strong winds can make high-altitude hikes dangerous.

6.2 When to See Wildflowers and Lush Greenery

Madeira's landscape is incredibly lush and vibrant throughout the year, but the best time to witness wildflowers in full bloom and the island's greenery at its peak is during the spring months of March to June.

During this period, Madeira's famous Laurisilva forests—especially areas like Levada do Caldeirão Verde, Levada do Rei, and Fanal Forest—become even more breathtaking, with fresh green foliage, misty atmospheres, and waterfalls at their fullest. The Levadas das 25 Fontes and Levada do Alecrim are particularly spectacular in spring, as the winter rains have replenished their water sources, creating stunning cascades.

Wildflowers begin to bloom in March and April, covering the meadows of Paul da Serra and Ponta de São Lourenço with vibrant bursts of yellow, purple, and pink. Coastal trails such as Boca do Risco and Porto Moniz's cliffside paths are also dotted with bright-colored flowers, contrasting against the deep blue of the Atlantic Ocean.

By May and June, Madeira's countryside is at its most lush and fragrant, making it the perfect time for hikers who want to experience the island's full natural beauty. The Madeira Flower Festival, held in Funchal each May, celebrates this floral explosion, making it an excellent time to visit for nature lovers.

During summer (July–September), some of the lower-altitude areas begin to dry out, particularly on sun-exposed ridges and coastal trails, but the mountain forests remain cool and green.

Winter (November to February), while wetter, also has its advantages for lush landscapes. The island's waterfalls become more powerful, and the forests take on an intense emerald green, especially in the northern regions where rainfall is more frequent. However, higher elevations may be muddy and slippery, requiring careful navigation.

Best Trails for Wildflowers & Greenery:

Levada do Rei winds through a dense Laurisilva forest, where towering trees and ferns thrive in the cool, misty air. The sound of flowing water adds to the peaceful atmosphere.

In Fanal Forest, ancient moss-covered trees stand like ghostly figures, especially when fog drifts through, creating an almost otherworldly scene.

The path to Levada das 25 Fontes is lined with lush vegetation, leading to a stunning wall of waterfalls cascading into a clear pool, surrounded by vibrant greenery.

On Paul da Serra, spring transforms the high-altitude plateau into a sea of wildflowers, with rolling meadows offering sweeping views of the island's rugged landscape.

At Ponta de São Lourenço, bright coastal flowers contrast sharply with volcanic cliffs and the deep blue ocean, creating one of Madeira's most striking and colorful hikes.

6.3 Rainy Season Precautions for Levada Walks

During the rainy season in Madeira, which typically lasts from October to March, levada walks take on a completely different character. The island's waterfalls become more powerful, the forests appear even greener, and mist often rolls through the valleys, creating a dreamlike atmosphere. However, with this beauty comes additional challenges that hikers need to be aware of. Heavy rainfall can make trails slippery, increase the risk of landslides, and lead to sudden changes in weather conditions. Some levadas, particularly those with narrow paths and exposed sections, become significantly more dangerous after storms.

Before setting out on a levada walk during the rainy season, it is always important to check the weather forecast. Conditions in the mountains can change rapidly, and what starts as a clear morning can quickly turn into thick fog and rain. Certain trails, such as Levada do Rei and Levada dos Balcões, are generally safer choices in wet conditions because they are more sheltered and have wider paths. On the other hand, Levada do Caldeirão Verde and Levada das 25 Fontes can be more hazardous due to steep drop-offs and rockfall-prone areas.

Proper gear is essential for hiking safely during this time of year. Waterproof boots with a good grip are a must, as wet stone paths and muddy trails can be extremely slippery. A lightweight rain jacket, a backpack cover, and extra dry clothing can help keep hikers comfortable in case of unexpected downpours. Using hiking poles can also improve stability on wet terrain.

One of the biggest concerns during the rainy season is rockfalls and landslides, which can occur after prolonged rain. Some levadas may be temporarily closed due to these hazards, and it is always best to respect closure signs and avoid taking unnecessary risks. If a trail appears blocked by debris or unstable ground, turning back is the safest option. Solo hiking in remote areas during this season is not recommended, as emergency response may take longer in case of an accident.

Despite the challenges, levada during the rainy season can be an incredible experience. The forests of Madeira's Laurisilva, a UNESCO World Heritage site, become even more vibrant, and the sound of rushing water fills the air. For those who are prepared and take the necessary precautions, hiking during this time of year offers a unique and rewarding perspective of the island's natural beauty.

6.4 Summer vs. Winter Hiking:

Hiking in Madeira varies dramatically between summer and winter, each season offering distinct landscapes and conditions.

Summer (June to September) is the best time for clear views, dry trails, and stable weather. During this season, high-altitude trails such as Pico Ruivo to Pico do Arieiro and the dramatic cliffs of Ponta de São Lourenço offer some of the most breathtaking panoramic vistas. The Paul da Serra plateau, one of the island's highest areas, remains cool and pleasant even in the warmer months. However, lower-altitude trails, particularly those with little shade, can become quite hot. It is important to start hikes early in the morning, bring plenty of water, and wear sun protection to avoid overheating.

Winter (October to March) brings cooler temperatures, frequent rain, and a completely different atmosphere. The Laurisilva forest flourishes during this time, with trails like Levada do Rei and Levada das 25 Fontes becoming particularly lush. Waterfalls are at their strongest, and the island's greenery reaches its peak. However, the risk of fog, rain, and slippery paths increases, making some hikes unpredictable. Summit trails such as Pico Ruivo can be covered in dense mist, limiting visibility, while certain coastal paths may experience strong winds.

Chapter 7

Hiking Safety and Emergency Preparedness

7.1 Understanding Madeira's Weather Patterns

Hiking in Madeira demands an awareness of the island's rapidly shifting weather, which can transform a clear morning into a foggy, rain-soaked afternoon in a matter of hours. The coastal regions often bask in mild temperatures and steady sunshine, but venture inland or gain elevation, and the conditions change dramatically. The trade winds sweeping in from the Atlantic dictate much of Madeira's climate, carrying moisture-heavy clouds that drape over the northern slopes, nurturing the lush Laurisilva forest while leaving the southern coast drier.

This contrast means that while Funchal might be bathed in sunlight, hikers ascending to Pico Ruivo or navigating the dramatic ridges of Vereda do Areeiro might find themselves enveloped in thick mist, with visibility reduced to just a few feet. Even levada trails, seemingly sheltered by dense vegetation, can become treacherous after rainfall, with narrow paths turning slick and waterfalls swelling unpredictably. It's not uncommon for mornings to start with clear skies, luring hikers into a false sense of security, only for dense clouds to roll in by midday, obscuring exposed trails like Boca do Risco or Ponta de São Lourenço. Wind speed also plays a role, especially on high-altitude routes where strong gusts can challenge even experienced hikers. Given this unpredictability, checking weather forecasts before setting out is essential, but preparation goes beyond that—carrying waterproof gear, dressing in layers, and packing essentials such as sun protection and extra provisions can make the difference between a rewarding trek and an unexpected struggle against the elements. Madeira's beauty lies in its untamed nature, but respecting the island's weather patterns is key to exploring it safely.

7.2 Wildlife and Natural Hazards

Madeira's landscapes are breathtaking, but they also present their own set of challenges, from its rugged cliffs to the delicate balance of its ecosystems. Unlike mainland Europe, the island is free from large predators, yet the natural environment requires vigilance. The Laurisilva forests, a UNESCO World Heritage site, are home to endemic bird species such as the Madeira firecrest, its bright plumage flashing between ancient tree branches, while seabirds like the Cory's shearwater nest along the cliffs, their haunting calls echoing at dusk. But for hikers, it's often the smaller creatures that demand attention, particularly the processionary caterpillar, found in pine forests, whose fine hairs can cause severe skin irritation or allergic reactions if touched. In the wetter months, slippery moss-covered stones and fallen leaves can make even the most well-maintained levada paths hazardous, while strong winds turn narrow ridges into precarious crossings. Rockfalls are a real concern, particularly on trails carved into sheer cliffsides, such as the Caminho Real or Vereda da Ponta de São Lourenço, where erosion from wind and rain loosens stones above. Even more dangerous are flash floods, which can transform dry riverbeds into rushing torrents within minutes, catching unprepared hikers off guard. The levada network itself, while a marvel of engineering, can pose risks—some sections follow narrow ledges with sheer drops, requiring a steady foot and a head for heights. Madeira's raw beauty is what makes it such a sought-after hiking destination, but understanding its natural hazards, respecting trail conditions, and being prepared for the unexpected are essential for a safe and enjoyable journey.

7.3 Trail Conditions and Cliffside Safety

Madeira's trails weave through a landscape shaped by time and the raw power of nature, offering hikers both awe-inspiring scenery and significant challenges. The levadas, with their tranquil flowing water and lush green surroundings, might seem gentle at first glance, but many run along cliffs, requiring balance and a steady footing. Some are carved directly into the mountainsides, their narrow paths lined with moss-covered rock walls on one side and sheer drop-offs on the other. Even more daunting are the high-altitude routes, such as the rugged trek between Pico Ruivo and Pico do Arieiro, where exposed ridgelines leave hikers at the mercy of sudden wind gusts and shifting weather. Early morning mist can roll in without warning, shrouding paths in an eerie fog that obscures the view—and the trail itself. On cliffside sections, loose gravel and erosion make footing unpredictable, and after heavy rain, rockfalls can pose unexpected dangers. Certain trails, like Vereda da Ponta de São Lourenço, run along Madeira's dramatic coastal cliffs, where the unrelenting wind can make each step feel like a battle against nature itself. Navigating these trails requires patience, proper gear, and a keen awareness of the surroundings. Good hiking boots with a solid grip are essential, as are trekking poles for added stability on steep or slippery terrain. Taking a moment to assess conditions before proceeding—whether it's testing a rocky step for stability or checking for trail warnings—is not just smart but necessary. The key to hiking safely in Madeira is respect: respect for the terrain, respect for the weather, and respect for the limits of the human body in a landscape where nature always has the final say.

7.4 Emergency Contacts and Rescue Services

When the trails of Madeira take an unexpected turn, knowing how to respond can be the difference between a minor mishap and a serious situation. The island's dramatic terrain, while breathtaking, can become treacherous in an instant, and even the most experienced hikers can find themselves needing assistance. The first and most important lifeline in any emergency is dialing 112, the direct number for emergency services, which connects to rescue teams trained to handle accidents in remote and rugged areas. Madeira's Civil Protection Authority constantly monitors weather patterns and trail safety, issuing alerts for hazards like rockslides, sudden fog, and storm-related trail closures. In some cases, mountain rescue teams, supported by the fire department or the regional police, are deployed for more complex rescues, often relying on helicopters to reach stranded or injured hikers in inaccessible areas. However, cell service is not always reliable in deep valleys or along certain mountain passes, making it crucial to carry a fully charged phone, a power bank, and, if possible, a whistle or emergency beacon. Knowing the nearest exit points along a trail, as well as designated emergency shelters, adds another layer of preparedness. One of the simplest yet most effective safety measures is informing someone about the planned route and expected return time—this small step ensures that, if something goes wrong, help will be sent in time. Madeira's trails offer an adventure unlike any other, but they demand respect, caution, and preparation. In this wild and unpredictable landscape, being ready for the unexpected is just as important as the journey itself.

Chapter 8

Local Culture, Food and Activities

8.1 Traditional Madeiran Cuisine: Must-Try Foods

Madeira's cuisine is a reflection of the island itself—bold, rich in tradition, and deeply connected to the land and sea. Every dish tells a story of the island's history, shaped by Portuguese roots, African influences, and the bounty of the Atlantic Ocean. At the heart of Madeiran dining is espetada, a mouthwatering skewer of beef marinated in garlic, salt, and bay leaves, then grilled over open flames and often served hanging from a metal stand, dripping juices onto a side of crispy milho frito (fried cornmeal cubes). For seafood lovers, lapas grelhadas—grilled limpets sizzling in butter, garlic, and lemon—are a staple, often enjoyed by the ocean with a cold Coral beer in hand.

One of the island's most iconic flavors comes from its bread: bolo do caco. This soft, slightly chewy bread, cooked on a hot stone, is best enjoyed warm with garlic butter melting into its golden crust. It often accompanies meals but can also be turned into a sandwich stuffed with carne vinha d'alhos, a Christmas-season favorite where pork is marinated in wine and garlic before being fried to perfection. Another must-try is poncha, the island's signature drink, made from aguardente de cana (sugarcane rum), honey, and citrus juice—strong, sweet, and deceptively smooth.

Beyond the savory dishes, Madeira's subtropical climate makes it a paradise for exotic fruits. Markets overflow with passionfruit, custard apples, bananas, and the uniquely tangy banana-passionfruit hybrid known as banana-maracujá. Meanwhile, desserts like bolo de mel, a dense molasses cake spiced with cinnamon and cloves, offer a taste of centuries-old tradition, originally made using sugarcane syrup from the island's plantations. Whether sitting down to a feast in a rustic tasca or grabbing a bolo do caco sandwich from a street vendor, eating in Madeira is more than just a meal—it's a cultural experience that connects visitors to the island's soul, one bite at a time.

8.2 Local Handicrafts and Souvenirs

Madeira's traditional handicrafts are more than just souvenirs; they are a testament to centuries-old artistry passed down through generations. Among the most renowned is Madeira embroidery (bordado Madeira), a delicate and intricate craft that has been prized worldwide since the 19th century. Made by skilled artisans, these hand-stitched linens—ranging from tablecloths to fine clothing—are characterized by elegant floral patterns, meticulous cutwork, and unparalleled craftsmanship. Visitors can explore workshops in Funchal to witness this art form in progress and even purchase authentic pieces bearing a certification of origin.

Another unique craft is tapestry weaving, particularly in the rural town of Santo da Serra, where wool rugs and wall hangings are still handmade on traditional looms. Equally impressive is the island's wickerwork, crafted in the village of Camacha. Here, artisans shape locally grown willow branches into beautifully woven furniture, baskets, and decorative pieces—practical souvenirs that capture the rustic charm of Madeira. The island's rich volcanic soil also inspires pottery and ceramics, with many studios producing hand-painted tiles and clay figurines reflecting Madeira's landscapes and traditions.

For those looking for a taste of Madeira to take home, bottles of the famous Madeira wine are a must. Aged through a unique heating process, this fortified wine comes in a variety of styles, from dry to lusciously sweet, each telling the story of the island's winemaking heritage. Locally produced honey cake (bolo de mel), regional jams, and small bottles of poncha also make for flavorful mementos. Whether it's a finely embroidered linen, a wicker basket, or a bottle of aged Malvasia wine, these handcrafted goods serve as lasting reminders of Madeira's cultural richness and the dedication of its artisans.

8.3 Other Outdoor Adventures:

Madeira's dramatic landscape isn't just for hiking; it's a playground for adrenaline seekers who want to experience the island's natural wonders from new perspectives. Canyoning is one of the most exhilarating ways to explore Madeira's rugged interior, leading adventurers through deep gorges, cascading waterfalls, and hidden pools. Equipped with wetsuits, harnesses, and helmets, participants rappel down rock faces, jump into crystal-clear basins, and slide through narrow channels carved by centuries of water flow. Some of the best canyoning spots include Ribeira das Cales in the heart of the island and Ribeiro Frio, where lush greenery and flowing streams create a wild, untouched atmosphere.

For those who prefer the skies, paragliding offers an unforgettable view of Madeira's coastline and mountains. Launching from scenic take-off points like Madalena do Mar or Porto da Cruz, paragliders soar effortlessly above terraced hillsides, dramatic cliffs, and the vast Atlantic. With stable winds and breathtaking scenery, Madeira is a prime location for both beginner and experienced pilots looking to experience the thrill of flight while taking in a bird's-eye view of the island's diverse landscapes.

Beneath the waves, Madeira's underwater world is just as captivating. The island's clear waters, volcanic caves, and vibrant marine life make it a paradise for diving and snorkeling. The Garajau Marine Reserve, one of the best diving spots, is home to large groupers, moray eels, and even the occasional manta ray gliding through the depths. Wreck diving enthusiasts can explore the Pronto and Bowbelle, sunken ships that have become artificial reefs teeming with marine life.

Chapter 9

Festivals, Events, and Local Hiking Calendar

Madeira's festivals are more than just celebrations—they are a reflection of the island's deep-rooted traditions, love for nature, and lively spirit. Time your hiking adventure to coincide with these events, and you'll find yourself walking through landscapes transformed by flower displays, music-filled streets, and dazzling firework shows over the Atlantic. These festivals are a chance to see Madeira in its most vibrant state, where nature and culture blend seamlessly, offering an unforgettable experience beyond the trails.

9.1 Madeira Flower Festival (Spring)

Spring in Madeira is a spectacle in itself. The mountains and valleys awaken with color as wildflowers burst into bloom, making every hiking trail feel like a passage through a natural garden. But in April or May, the beauty of nature spills into the streets as the Madeira Flower Festival turns Funchal into a living work of art. This is not just a festival—it's an island-wide tribute to nature, tradition, and renewal. The moment you step into Funchal's historic center, the air is filled with the scent of fresh flowers. Enormous, intricately designed floral carpets stretch across city squares, their patterns reflecting Madeira's deep connection to its natural surroundings. The highlight of the festival is the grand parade, where floats covered in exotic blooms roll through the streets, led by dancers in elaborate flower-inspired costumes. The energy is contagious—local families and visitors alike gather to watch as musicians, folklore groups, and performers bring the streets to life.

One of the most moving traditions is the **"Wall of Hope"** ceremony, where children place flowers on a symbolic wall, representing a collective wish for peace in the world. For those who love nature, this event goes beyond spectacle—it is a reminder of the island's rich biodiversity and the way flowers have become a central part of its identity. For hikers, spring is already one of the best seasons to explore Madeira's landscapes, and the Flower Festival only enhances the experience. Trails such as Levada do Rei and Levada das 25 Fontes are at their most lush, with waterfalls flowing strongly and the forests of Laurisilva thriving in shades of green. The high-altitude plains of Paul da Serra become a tapestry of wildflowers, while the valleys near Rabaçal are alive with blooming hydrangeas and lilies. After a morning hike, returning to Funchal for an afternoon filled with floral art, music, and celebrations feels like a perfect balance of adventure and culture.

9.2 Atlantic Festival (Summer)

As spring fades into summer, Madeira's nights come alive with a different kind of spectacle—the Atlantic

Festival, held throughout June. If the Flower Festival is a celebration of nature's beauty, the Atlantic Festival is an ode to energy, creativity, and light. Each weekend, the skies over Funchal Bay explode in fireworks, synchronized to music in a thrilling competition between international pyrotechnic teams. The entire city turns its attention to the harbor, where crowds gather along the waterfront, eyes fixed on the sky as bursts of color reflect over the Atlantic.

For those who love both adventure and nightlife, this is an ideal time to visit. The long daylight hours allow for full-day hikes in the mountains before descending into town for an evening of festivities. A perfect itinerary might start with an early morning trek along the Ponta de São Lourenço, where the golden summer light illuminates the rugged coastline. The heat of the afternoon could be spent exploring shaded levada walks, such as Levada do Alecrim, where the sound of running water offers a refreshing contrast to the sun-soaked cliffs. And as dusk falls, there's no better place to be than the marina in Funchal, with a cool drink in hand, waiting for the fireworks to paint the night sky. Beyond the pyrotechnic displays, the festival also brings concerts, dance performances, and open-air events to various parts of the city. The streets fill with a mix of classical and modern music, from orchestral symphonies to lively folk groups playing traditional braguinha guitars. Many restaurants and bars host special events, offering visitors a chance to enjoy Madeiran cuisine in a festive atmosphere. Summer hiking in Madeira comes with its own set of experiences. The sun casts long, golden hues over the Encumeada Pass, and the high-altitude plateaus of Paul da Serra offer panoramic views that stretch to the ocean. Evenings remain warm, making it easy to explore beyond the trails, whether it's strolling along the historic streets of Funchal or joining the lively crowds gathered to watch the fireworks competitions. The Atlantic Festival is a time when Madeira is at its most dynamic, offering the perfect blend of adventure and celebration.

9.3 Madeira Wine Festival (Late Summer)

As the golden hues of late summer settle over Madeira, the island bursts into a celebration of its most treasured tradition—the Madeira Wine Festival. Walking through the streets of Funchal in early September, you're instantly swept up in the rich aroma of fermenting grapes, the sounds of folk music echoing through the city, and the lively chatter of locals sharing their passion for winemaking. The festival is more than just a showcase of Madeira's world-famous fortified wine; it's a tribute to centuries of hard work, craftsmanship, and the deep-rooted connection between the island and its vineyards.

The heart of the festival beats strongest in Estreito de Câmara de Lobos, where the traditional grape harvest and stomping rituals bring visitors face-to-face with an age-old practice. Here, barefoot participants step into large wooden barrels, pressing the freshly picked grapes beneath their feet, just as generations of winemakers have done before them. The experience is as authentic as it gets—laughter fills the air, traditional bailinho da Madeira dancers twirl to the rhythm of folk songs, and the scent of freshly crushed grapes lingers long after you've left the vineyard. Back in Funchal, Avenida Arriaga is transformed into an open-air market where stalls overflow with Madeira's finest wines. The opportunity to sample everything from the crisp, dry Sercial to the rich, sweet Malmsey is an experience no visitor should miss. Expert winemakers guide you through the tasting process, offering insights into the unique characteristics of each varietal. Nearby, street performers in traditional Madeiran costumes reenact the island's winemaking history, while local artisans showcase handcrafted cork products, embroidery, and pottery, making it the perfect place to pick up a meaningful souvenir. As evening falls, the city becomes a stage for historical parades and live performances. Costumed actors bring Madeira's 15th-century wine trade to life, depicting the days when barrels of wine were loaded onto ships bound for faraway markets. The grand parade, a highlight of the festival, sees elaborately decorated floats glide through the streets, each representing a different region of Madeira's wine industry. Under the glow of lanterns and the warmth of late summer air, the festival feels like a journey back in time, one where tradition and celebration intertwine seamlessly.

For those eager to explore Madeira's vineyards beyond the festival, the best way to do so is on foot. Trails like Levada do Norte, weaving through the terraced hillsides of Câmara de Lobos, offer sweeping views of the island's rolling vineyards. Meanwhile, the São Vicente Valley Walk, nestled in one of Madeira's lushest wine-growing regions, allows hikers to experience the island's agricultural beauty up close. Whether sipping a glass of fine Madeira wine in Funchal's bustling streets or walking through the quiet, vine-covered landscapes, the festival provides an unforgettable immersion into the island's most cherished tradition.

9.4 Christmas and New Year's Fireworks (Winter)

Winter in Madeira may not bring snow, but it transforms the island into a dazzling spectacle of light, music, and festivity. From the moment December begins, Funchal is illuminated by thousands of twinkling Christmas lights, casting a warm glow over the city's historic streets. A stroll through Avenida Arriaga feels like stepping into a holiday postcard—wooden market stalls overflow with handcrafted decorations, the scent of roasted chestnuts fills the air, and musicians play cheerful carols beneath the glow of festive lanterns. It's a season of togetherness, where both locals and visitors come together to celebrate Madeira's unique blend of tradition and holiday magic.

As Christmas Eve approaches, families gather for an evening filled with Carne Vinha d'Alhos, a traditional dish of marinated pork, garlic, and wine, prepared days in advance for the special occasion. The night culminates with Missa do Galo (Midnight Mass), held in churches across the island, where the faithful light candles and sing hymns that echo through the valleys. In the smaller villages, beautifully arranged Lapinha nativity scenes are displayed outside homes, a testament to Madeira's deep-rooted religious customs. But nothing compares to the grandeur of New Year's Eve in Funchal, home to one of the world's most spectacular fireworks displays. As midnight approaches, anticipation fills the air. Whether you're standing along the Funchal Marina, watching from a viewpoint like Pico dos Barcelos, or aboard one of the many New Year's Eve cruises that set sail for the occasion, the moment is unforgettable. Then, as the clock strikes twelve, the sky erupts into an explosion of color. The fireworks—recognized by the Guinness World Records as one of the largest synchronized displays on the planet—illuminate the entire bay, reflecting off the water and painting the city in vibrant hues. It's a breathtaking sight, a moment where time seems to stand still as the new year is welcomed with awe and excitement.

For those eager to pair the festivities with adventure, Madeira's winter hiking trails offer an incredible contrast to the season's celebrations. The Vereda dos Balcões trail, a short but scenic walk, is perfect for a quiet morning before the holiday buzz sets in. Meanwhile, the Ponta de São Lourenço hike, with its dramatic cliffs and untamed coastline, is ideal for those seeking crisp winter air and solitude before rejoining the festivities. Whether you come for the lights, the traditions, or the fireworks that light up the Atlantic sky, Madeira in winter is nothing short of magical.

9.5 Local Trail-Running and Hiking Events

Beyond its festivals, Madeira is a paradise for outdoor enthusiasts, offering some of the most thrilling trail-running and hiking events in Europe. One of the most renowned is the Madeira Island Ultra Trail (MIUT), held each April. This grueling race spans 115 kilometers, taking runners across the island's highest peaks, from Porto Moniz to Machico. The challenge is as mental as it is physical, with participants navigating rocky ridges, misty forests, and steep ascents under the shifting weather conditions of Madeira's unpredictable microclimates.

For those looking for something more accessible, the Ecotrail Funchal, held in October, combines urban exploration with rugged nature trails. Participants run through Funchal's botanical gardens, past historic landmarks, and into the surrounding mountains, with distances ranging from 15 kilometers to 85 kilometers. Meanwhile, the Madeira Walking Festival in January invites hikers of all levels to experience guided walks through the island's most breathtaking trails, from gentle levada strolls to demanding mountain treks. Even Madeira's sister island, Porto Santo, gets in on the action with the Porto Santo Nature Trail in November. This event, featuring 10-kilometer, 21-kilometer, and 42-kilometer distances, takes runners across golden beaches and volcanic landscapes, offering a different but equally stunning take on Madeira's natural beauty.

Chapter 10

Environmental Responsibility and Hiking Ethics

Hiking in Madeira offers breathtaking landscapes, from misty laurel forests to rugged coastal cliffs, but with its beauty comes the responsibility to preserve these fragile environments. The island's ecosystem is home to rare plant species, endemic wildlife, and delicate geological formations that have been shaped over millions of years. Every step along a levada or mountain trail should be taken with care, ensuring that future generations can experience the same pristine beauty. Understanding and following responsible hiking ethics is essential, not just as a guideline but as a commitment to protecting Madeira's natural heritage.

10.1 Leave No Trace:

Madeira's natural environment is exceptionally diverse, but it is also sensitive to human impact. Practicing Leave No Trace (LNT) principles ensures that hikers minimize their footprint while exploring the island's trails.

- Pack out all waste—even biodegradable items like fruit peels and nutshells, which can disrupt the ecosystem and attract animals to non-natural food sources.

- Stay on marked trails to prevent erosion and protect fragile vegetation, particularly in high-altitude areas like Pico Ruivo and Paul da Serra, where plant life is slow to recover from damage.
- Avoid disturbing wildlife by observing from a distance and never feeding birds or small mammals, as human food can alter their natural behavior.
- Be mindful of water sources, refraining from contaminating streams and levadas with soap, sunscreen, or waste.
- Camp only in designated areas, as wild camping is strictly regulated to prevent damage to the environment.

10.2 Rules for Hiking in Protected Areas

Many of Madeira's trails pass through protected reserves, including the Laurisilva Forest, a UNESCO World Heritage Site, and the Garajau Nature Reserve, home to marine life and seabird colonies. Hiking in these areas comes with specific regulations to safeguard biodiversity.

1. Permits may be required for certain trails, such as those passing through highly sensitive zones. Always check ahead with local authorities or park management.

2. Dogs and pets are often restricted to avoid disturbing wildlife. Before setting out, confirm whether the area allows animals.

3. Open fires and barbecues are prohibited in protected forests due to the high risk of wildfires, particularly during the dry summer months.

4. Noise pollution should be kept to a minimum—loud music or shouting can disturb animals and diminish the natural experience for other hikers.

5. Collecting plants, rocks, or other natural items is not allowed, as removing them disrupts the ecosystem. Rangers and local conservationists actively monitor these areas, ensuring that visitors respect regulations designed to preserve Madeira's stunning landscapes.

By embracing environmental responsibility and respecting the rules of protected areas, hikers can enjoy Madeira's trails while playing a role in conservation efforts. The island's natural beauty is a privilege to experience, and it is up to every visitor to ensure that it remains unspoiled for generations to come.

10.3 Responsible Waste Disposal

Proper waste disposal is one of the most crucial aspects of responsible hiking in Madeira. While the island's trails take you through untouched landscapes, even small traces of human activity can have long-lasting effects on the environment.

- Always carry a waste bag to pack out everything you bring, including food wrappers, tissues, and organic waste like fruit peels, which take longer to decompose in certain climates.

- Use designated trash and recycling bins where available, but be prepared to take your waste with you, as many remote trails lack disposal facilities.
- Avoid single-use plastics by bringing a reusable water bottle and food containers. Madeira's natural springs and some levadas provide drinkable water, but always check for safety before refilling.
- Toilet waste should be managed carefully—use restrooms before starting your hike, and if nature calls on the trail, follow Leave No Trace principles by digging a small hole at least 60 meters away from water sources and covering it properly.
- Be mindful of cigarette butts, which are not only litter but also pose a significant wildfire risk. Carry a portable ashtray if needed. A clean trail ensures that both nature and future hikers can continue to enjoy Madeira's landscapes without the negative impact of waste.

10.4 Supporting Local Conservation Efforts

Preserving Madeira's hiking trails and rich biodiversity requires the collective effort of visitors, locals, and conservation groups. There are many ways hikers can contribute to the protection of these natural spaces.

- Participate in organized clean-up hikes, which are occasionally led by environmental organizations and local hiking groups—these initiatives help remove litter from trails and levadas while educating participants on conservation challenges.
- Support eco-conscious businesses and tour operators that prioritize sustainability, such as those using electric vehicles for transportation or following ethical wildlife-watching practices.
- Donate to or volunteer with local conservation projects, such as those focused on reforestation or the protection of endangered species like the Madeiran long-toed pigeon.
- Respect conservation zones and follow regulations to minimize human impact—staying on marked paths, avoiding trampling on vegetation, and adhering to guidelines in national parks all contribute to preservation efforts.
- Educate others about responsible hiking by sharing best practices with fellow travelers and encouraging sustainable tourism. Every small action counts in maintaining Madeira's natural beauty, ensuring that its unique ecosystems continue to thrive for generations to come.

Chapter 11

Practical Travel Tips

Planning a hiking trip to Madeira involves more than just choosing trails—it's about understanding the island's practical details to ensure a smooth and enjoyable journey. From managing daily expenses to communicating with locals, knowing how to navigate the essentials makes every step of the adventure more comfortable. Madeira's hospitality blends seamlessly with its natural beauty, but having the right information at hand allows visitors to immerse themselves fully in the island's culture and landscapes.

11.1 Currency and Payment Methods

Madeira, like the rest of Portugal, uses the Euro (€) as its official currency. Cash is widely accepted, especially in small villages, local markets, and rural areas where card payment options might be limited. While credit and debit cards are commonly used in hotels, supermarkets, and larger restaurants in cities like Funchal, smaller establishments along hiking routes often prefer cash. It's advisable to carry small denominations of euros to pay for snacks, coffee, or transportation in more remote locations.

ATMs, known locally as Multibanco, are widely available in towns and villages, allowing visitors to withdraw cash easily. However, some isolated areas may not have nearby cash machines, making it essential to plan withdrawals ahead of long hikes. Contactless payments and mobile apps like Apple Pay and Google Pay are increasingly accepted in urban areas, but hikers should not rely solely on digital methods when exploring remote trails.

Tipping is not obligatory in Madeira, but is appreciated for good service. In restaurants, rounding up the bill or leaving 5–10% is customary. For guided hikes or tours, tipping is a kind gesture if the service has been helpful and informative. By preparing a mix of payment methods, hikers can ensure they're ready for any situation, whether stopping at a local café after a long trek or purchasing souvenirs from village artisans.

11.2 Language and Useful Portuguese Phrases for Hikers

The official language in Madeira is Portuguese, and while many people in Funchal and tourist areas speak English, venturing into smaller villages or rural trails may require basic communication in Portuguese. Learning a few essential phrases not only helps with practical needs but also shows respect for local culture, often opening the door to more friendly interactions.

Simple greetings like "Bom dia" **(Good morning)** or "Boa tarde" **(Good afternoon)** go a long way in creating a warm connection with locals. When asking for directions, phrases like "Onde fica o trilho?" **(Where is the trail?)** or "Quanto tempo até o destino?" **(How long**

to the destination?) can be particularly helpful on less marked routes.

For hikers exploring remote areas, knowing how to request assistance or necessities is vital. "Preciso de água" **(I need water)** or "Há algum café aqui perto?" **(Is there a café nearby?)** can be useful during long treks. In case of emergencies, "Preciso de ajuda" **(I need help)** or "Chame uma ambulância" **(Call an ambulance)** can be life-saving phrases to communicate with locals or emergency services.

Most signs along hiking trails use international symbols or are marked in both Portuguese and English, especially on popular routes. However, locals often appreciate when visitors make the effort to speak their language, even if only a few words. Carrying a small phrasebook or downloading a translation app can be a valuable tool for navigating conversations on the trail or in small villages.

11.3 Mobile Networks and Wi-Fi Access

Staying connected while hiking in Madeira depends largely on the location. Urban areas like Funchal, Machico, and Câmara de Lobos offer strong mobile network coverage and widespread Wi-Fi access in cafes, hotels, and public spaces. However, once hikers venture into remote trails, deep valleys, or high-altitude routes, network signals can become weak or disappear entirely.

The main mobile operators in Madeira are MEO, NOS, and Vodafone, all of which provide 4G and some 5G coverage in populated areas. Tourists from the EU can use Roam Like at Home, meaning they won't face additional roaming charges. For non-EU visitors, purchasing a local SIM card at the airport or in Funchal can be a cost-effective way to stay connected.

Wi-Fi is widely available in hotels, restaurants, and visitor centers, but hikers should not rely on it when out on the trails. Those planning multi-day hikes or venturing into remote levadas should download offline maps and ensure their phones are fully charged. Carrying a portable power bank can be a lifesaver when navigating long routes.

For emergencies, even if there is no signal for calls, sending a text message (SMS) or using emergency apps can sometimes work in low-signal areas. It's always a good idea to inform someone about hiking plans before setting off, especially in isolated regions where communication may be limited.

11.4 Local Hiking Laws and Regulations

Madeira takes the conservation of its trails and natural parks seriously, and hikers are expected to follow local regulations to ensure safety and environmental protection. Many of the island's best trails, such as Levada das 25 Fontes and Pico do Arieiro to Pico Ruivo, pass through protected areas like the Madeira Natural Park and the Laurisilva Forest, a UNESCO World Heritage Site.

Stick to Official Trails – Off-trail hiking is not allowed in many areas to protect fragile ecosystems and prevent accidents. Trails are well-marked, and wandering off can be both dangerous and damaging to the environment.

Group Size Limits – Some trails have restrictions on the maximum number of hikers allowed per group to reduce environmental impact. If hiring a guide, check whether permits or reservations are needed for certain routes.

Camping Rules – Wild camping is not permitted in Madeira's natural parks. Hikers looking to camp must stay at designated camping sites and follow all regulations regarding waste disposal and fire safety.

Fires and Smoking – Due to the risk of wildfires, making fires or smoking on trails is strictly prohibited, especially in dry seasons. The island enforces heavy fines for violations.

Respect Weather Warnings – Authorities issue trail closure notices due to landslides, heavy rain, or strong winds. Always check local weather updates and Madeira's Civil Protection website before heading out.

No Unauthorized Drone Use – Flying drones is restricted in natural parks, coastal cliffs, and UNESCO areas. Special permits are required for drone photography in many locations.

Chapter 12.

Recommended Itineraries

12.1 One-Day Hikes for Short Visits

For travelers with only a single day to explore, choosing the right trail is crucial. A perfect option is Levada do Caldeirão Verde, a scenic 13-kilometer (8-mile) route that winds through the UNESCO-listed Laurisilva forest, past waterfalls, and into deep green valleys. The trail is moderately challenging but rewards hikers with one of the most stunning levada experiences on the island. Another excellent choice is Ponta de São Lourenço, a 7-kilometer (4.3-mile) out-and-back hike showcasing Madeira's rugged eastern coastline, with striking volcanic rock formations and panoramic Atlantic views. This hike is relatively short but offers some of the most dramatic scenery on the island. For those who prefer a high-altitude challenge, Pico do Arieiro to Pico Ruivo is an unforgettable 11-kilometer (6.8-mile) ridge hike linking two of Madeira's highest peaks. The route involves steep ascents and descents, but the breathtaking cloud-covered peaks and sweeping vistas make it one of the most rewarding short hikes.

12.2 Three-Day Itinerary for a Weekend Hiking Adventure

Day 1: Coastal and Forest Exploration

Begin with the Levada das 25 Fontes, a 9-kilometer (5.6-mile) trek through lush vegetation and cascading waterfalls. The well-maintained trail is one of the island's most famous, offering a deep dive into Madeira's rich biodiversity. In the afternoon, take a short drive to Fanal Forest, where ancient, mist-shrouded laurel trees create an almost mystical atmosphere. This area is perfect for a leisurely walk and a picnic before heading back to town.

Day 2: Mountain Peaks and Sunrise Views

Wake up early for a sunrise hike to Pico Ruivo, Madeira's highest peak at 1,862 meters (6,109 feet). Starting from Achada do Teixeira, the 5.4-kilometer (3.3-mile) round-trip hike offers unparalleled mountain views. After descending, visit the charming town of Santana to explore its traditional thatched houses and enjoy a hearty Madeiran meal.

Day 3: Dramatic Coastal Cliffs

On the final day, take on the Vereda da Ponta de São Lourenço, a moderate coastal hike where towering cliffs drop steeply into the ocean. The striking contrast of volcanic rock, bright wildflowers, and the deep blue sea makes this a spectacular way to end the adventure. If time allows, a swim at the Prainha beach or a boat tour along the coastline can add a refreshing end to the trip.

12.3 Seven-Day Itinerary for Exploring Madeira's Best Trails

Spending a full week hiking in Madeira offers the kind of rewarding journey that unfolds gradually with each day, revealing the layered beauty of the island—its coastlines, forests, highlands, and tucked-away villages. This itinerary is designed to take in some of Madeira's most well-known hiking routes without rushing, combining the thrill of difficult ascents with opportunities to slow down, recover, and appreciate the subtleties of the environment and local life.

Day One: Arrival and Coastal Exploration

As soon as I landed, I headed to Madeira's eastern edge for a more relaxed start. The trail at Vereda da Ponta de São Lourenço was a suitable introduction to the island's terrain. The 7 km (4.3-mile) out-and-back route follows the narrow peninsula, with waves crashing below and sculpted volcanic cliffs stretching ahead. The land here is dry and windblown, in stark contrast to the lush interior I'd discover later in the week. After the hike, I returned to Funchal, wandered through the old town's cobblestone streets, and finished the evening with a plate of grilled black scabbardfish and a glass of Madeira wine—simple, fresh, and just what I needed.

Day two: Laurisilva Forest and Waterfalls.

The following morning, we drove into the misty mountains to hike Levada do Caldeirão Verde. This 13-

kilometre (8-mile) levada trail led me deep into the Laurisilva forest, a UNESCO World Heritage Site known for its unique ecosystem. Ferns brushed against my legs as the trail wound through damp tunnels and past waterfalls that seemed to emerge unexpectedly from the moss-covered cliffs. After lunch, I headed to Fanal Forest. In the fog, centuries-old laurel trees stood gnarled and still, their silhouettes reminiscent of a storybook. The silence in this forest was unlike anything I'd heard before; it was almost as if the trees were listening.

Day 3: High peaks and breathtaking views.

This was the most difficult day, but it was also the one I had anticipated the most. I set out before dawn for the trail that connects Pico do Arieiro to Pico Ruivo, a difficult 11 km (6.8 miles) trek through the central mountains. The staircases carved into the volcanic rock, the narrow ridges, and the tunnels that cut through the mountain walls provided an unforgettable experience. The views changed dramatically with each turn, from jagged peaks shrouded in clouds to wide-open panoramas with the coast visible on both sides. Reaching Pico Ruivo, the island's highest point at 1,862 meters (6,109 feet), felt like being on top of the world.

Day Four: Relaxation and Short Scenic Trails

After the mountainous exertion, I welcomed the slower pace. I travelled to Porto Moniz in the northwest to soak in the natural lava pools, which were the ideal remedy for tired legs. Floating in the saltwater as waves crashed just beyond the walls felt like a well-deserved reward. Later that afternoon, I embarked on the Levada do Rei, a tranquil and shady 10 km (6.2 miles) path lined with lush vegetation and bird song. There was just enough movement to keep the rhythm going without pushing too hard.

Day 5: 25 Waterfalls and Hidden Valleys

This day was all about water and greenery. I hiked the well-known Levada das 25 Fontes, which includes a detour to Risco Waterfall, for a total of 9 km (5.6 miles) of cascading water, laurel forest, and steep, fern-covered cliffs. Although the trail can be congested, the abundance of waterfalls and lush scenery makes every step worthwhile. Later, I made my way to Jardim do Mar, a small coastal village that appeared to be frozen in time. I sat in a quiet café overlooking the sea, watching surfers ride late afternoon waves.

Day 6: Remote Villages and Authentic Madeira

This morning began with a quieter, lesser-known walk along the Levada do Moinho-Levada Nova trail. It's about 8 kilometres (5 miles) long, and while it's not as well-known as other hikes, it provides expansive views of terraced fields and tiny hamlets that cling to the slopes. The sense of immersion into local life was stronger here, with chickens in backyards, smoke curling from chimneys, and farmers working the land by hand. In the afternoon, I visited São Vicente. The Grutas de São Vicente (lava tubes) show how Madeira's volcanic base was formed. It is based on geological experience, connecting the dots between the peaks, forests, and the sea.

Day 7: Sunrise, Farewell, and Departure

Before heading to the airport, I took one last walk, brief but meaningful. I hiked 5.4 kilometres (3.3 miles) round-trip from Achada do Teixeira to Pico Ruivo, this time to see the sunrise. The morning air was cold and still, and the trail was quiet. I reached the summit just as the sun broke over the horizon, casting golden light across the jagged ridges. Standing there again, knowing I was leaving soon, gave me a quiet sense of closure. It was the ideal way to cap off a week that had provided so much more than just trails—it left me with a lasting connection to a place shaped by wind, water, and history.

12.4 Custom itineraries for families, solo hikers, and groups

Madeira provides a diverse range of hiking experiences for all types of travelers. The island's well-maintained trail network allows visitors to create itineraries that match their interests and abilities, from short scenic walks ideal for young children to longer, more challenging routes that appeal to experienced solo hikers or active groups. Below are a few sample plans tailored to specific types of hikers: families with children, solo travelers seeking adventure, and hiking groups or friends visiting together.

For families with children.

This family-friendly itinerary emphasizes short and safe trails, scenic views, educational stops, and relaxing outdoor settings. The goal is to keep each day engaging and enjoyable for children without being overly strenuous.

Day 1: Vereda dos Balcões (3 km, 1.8 miles).

Vereda dos Balcões, located in Ribeiro Frio, is a flat and easy-to-follow trail. It follows a short section of levada through the Laurisilva forest before ending at a panoramic viewpoint overlooking central Madeira's deep valleys. It's a peaceful walk suitable for all ages, with opportunities to see native birds and enjoy panoramic views.

Day 2: Levada do Rei (10 kilometres or 6.2 miles)

Levada do Rei, near São Jorge, is a shaded and well-maintained trail through lush green vegetation. It is longer than the previous walk, but with a gentle profile and plenty of rest stops, it is suitable for older children or active younger ones. The trail also goes through tunnels and past small waterfalls, keeping younger hikers interested throughout.

Day 3: São Vicente Caves and Porto Moniz Natural Pools.

This day transitions from hiking to a mix of light exploration and enjoyment. The São Vicente caves provide a guided tour through lava tubes, adding a geological element to the experience. In the afternoon, Porto Moniz's natural volcanic pools offer safe and shallow swimming areas. It's a fun and relaxing way to end a family-friendly visit.

For solo hikers seeking adventure.

Solo hikers frequently seek personal challenges, breathtaking scenery, and solitude in nature. This itinerary combines iconic, high-reward hikes with quieter trails ideal for reflection and self-paced travel.

Day 1: Pico do Arieiro to Pico Ruivo.

This challenging point-to-point trail connects Madeira's second and highest peaks. It includes steep ascents and descents, rock-cut stairways, and narrow ridge crossings. Despite the difficulty, the panoramic views and dramatic terrain make it one of the most visually appealing hikes on the island. This route is best attempted early in the day, when conditions are stable.

Day 2: Levada das 25 Fontes

This popular but rewarding levada walk follows narrow irrigation channels through dense forest before ending in a basin with multiple waterfalls trickling down a mossy cliff. Despite its popularity, the scenery and natural beauty remain the highlights. Going early in the morning or late in the afternoon reduces crowds.

Day 3: Vereda da Ponta do São Lourenço.

Located on the island's eastern peninsula, this trail provides a dramatic change in scenery. It travels over volcanic ridges with steep drop-offs on either side and uninterrupted views of the ocean. It's an excellent coastal hike for those who enjoy dramatic scenery and want to discover another side of Madeira's natural environment.

Day 4: Levada do Moinho

Levada do Moinho is quieter and less crowded, providing a more introspective experience. The trail goes through terraced fields, rustic stone houses, and forested slopes. With fewer hikers around, there are more opportunities for solitude and a slower, more deliberate pace. This route is especially popular among those looking for less commercialized trails.

For groups of friends or hiking clubs.

Groups benefit from trails that allow for conversation, shared moments, and moderate challenge levels that can accommodate a variety of abilities. This itinerary combines scenic group hikes with cultural experiences and relaxation.

Day 1: Pico Ruivo Sunrise Hike (via Achada do Teixeira)

This is a brief but inspirational hike to Madeira's highest point. Starting from Achada do Teixeira, the well-marked trail gradually ascends to the summit. It's a popular sunrise hike because of the clear views and shorter distance, making it ideal for larger groups and those looking to get a good start to their trip.

Day 2: Walk to Caldeirão Verde

This 13 km route is ideal for group hikes. The trail winds through lush Laurisilva forest, along cliffs, and through small tunnels carved into the rock. It ends at the Caldeirão Verde waterfall. The trail's varied scenery and moderate difficulty make it ideal for hiking clubs and groups.

Day 3: Porto Moniz and Fanal Forest.

This day combines a visit to the Fanal forest—a cloudy, misty area with ancient laurel trees—with a stop in the coastal village of Porto Moniz to balance active hiking with more relaxed exploration. The forest has short, photogenic trails, and you can spend the afternoon swimming, relaxing, or exploring the coast. This split-day plan provides flexibility for groups with diverse interests.

Chapter 13

Additional Resources

A well-prepared hiker understands that knowledge is just as crucial as sturdy boots or a reliable map. Madeira's trails, with their ever-changing conditions and diverse landscapes, require careful planning and up-to-date information. Whether you're looking for real-time trail updates, expert insights, or a community of fellow explorers, having access to the right resources can significantly enhance your experience. From trusted hiking websites and apps to local hiking groups and social media accounts, this section compiles the best tools available to ensure your time on the island's trails is both safe and rewarding.

13.1 Recommended Hiking Websites and Apps

In today's digital world, having reliable hiking apps and websites at your fingertips can make all the difference when planning your routes or navigating the trails. One of the most popular platforms among hikers is AllTrails, which provides detailed trail maps, user reviews, GPS tracking, and elevation profiles. This app is especially useful for gauging trail difficulty and finding hidden gems recommended by other hikers. For those who prefer a resource dedicated specifically to Madeira, WalkMe Madeira is an invaluable tool. This app offers offline maps, route descriptions, and essential safety information tailored to the island's unique network of levadas and mountain paths.

Another highly recommended app is Maps.me, which allows you to download detailed offline maps—an essential feature when venturing into remote areas with limited or no cell service. When it comes to weather forecasting, Windy and Meteo Madeira provide highly accurate predictions, including wind speeds and cloud cover—critical details for high-altitude hikes like the Pico Ruivo trek. Additionally, checking the Madeira Tourism Board's official website before heading out can help you stay informed about any trail closures or maintenance work, ensuring a smooth and hassle-free hiking experience.

13.2 Local Hiking Clubs and Groups

Joining a local hiking club or group can transform your experience, offering opportunities to meet like-minded adventurers and gain deeper insight into Madeira's landscapes. One of the most established organizations is Clube de Montanha do Funchal, which regularly organizes guided hikes, mountaineering activities, and conservation projects. Their events cater to all levels, from leisurely walks through lush levadas to demanding summit climbs for experienced trekkers.

For those looking for a more social and interactive experience, guided hiking groups like Madeira Adventure Kingdom and Explore Madeira Hiking provide well-organized excursions led by knowledgeable local guides. These hikes go beyond navigation—they include fascinating insights into Madeira's rich history, diverse plant life, and unique geological formations.

If you prefer a more flexible approach, online communities such as Hiking in Madeira and Madeira Outdoor Adventures on Facebook offer a great platform to connect with fellow hikers, share trail updates, and ask for recommendations. These groups often provide real-time information on weather conditions, trail difficulties, and any recent changes, making them an invaluable resource for both visitors and locals.

13.3 Best Social Media Accounts for Trail Updates

Social media has become an essential tool for hikers, providing real-time trail updates, route inspiration, and a space to engage with fellow adventurers. On Instagram, accounts like @discovermadeira and @madeiraislandhikes showcase breathtaking images of Madeira's trails, while also sharing valuable hiking tips and recommended routes. These pages serve as both inspiration and a practical guide for choosing the best hikes suited to your experience level.

For those who prefer video content, YouTube channels such as Madeira Hiking Trails offer detailed trail walkthroughs, stunning drone footage, and step-by-step guides to some of the island's most scenic routes. Watching these videos before a hike can provide a clearer idea of the terrain, difficulty level, and highlights along the way, ensuring that you're well-prepared for what lies ahead.

Facebook pages like Madeira Weather and Trails frequently post updates on trail conditions, closures, and weather warnings—essential information for planning safe and enjoyable hikes. Additionally, Twitter accounts managed by local authorities, such as the Instituto das Florestas e Conservação da Natureza (IFCN), provide official announcements on environmental protection measures and trail accessibility.

Chapter 14

Final Thoughts

Reaching the end of this guide is just the beginning of your adventure in Madeira. The island's trails offer an experience that goes beyond the physical act of hiking—they immerse you in landscapes shaped by time, culture, and the forces of nature. From the misty laurel forests of Fanal to the dramatic peaks of Pico Ruivo and the serene levadas winding through lush valleys, each path tells a story waiting to be discovered. Whether you are drawn to Madeira for the challenge of its rugged terrain or the tranquillity of its coastal walks, the key to a rewarding experience lies in preparation, awareness, and a willingness to embrace the unexpected. As you step onto these trails, it's important to carry not just the right gear but also an appreciation for the land, respect for its natural beauty, and a mindset open to adventure.

14.1 Tips for First-Time Visitors

If this is your first-time hiking in Madeira, there are a few things you should know to ensure a smooth and enjoyable experience. First and foremost, understand that Madeira's trails can vary significantly in difficulty and conditions. A trail that appears easy on paper may involve steep climbs, narrow ridges, or long descents that challenge your endurance. Research your route thoroughly and always check the latest trail conditions, as landslides and temporary closures are common, especially in remote areas.

Weather can change rapidly, particularly at higher altitudes, so dressing in layers is essential. Mornings might start with clear skies, but by midday, dense fog or sudden rain showers can roll in, affecting visibility and trail safety. Waterproof clothing and sturdy hiking boots with good grip are non-negotiable, as many paths can be slippery, especially after rain. Carrying enough water is also crucial, as not all trails have accessible refill points, and dehydration can set in quickly, particularly on exposed routes.

Respect for nature and trail etiquette goes a long way in preserving the beauty of Madeira's landscapes. Stick to marked paths to avoid damaging fragile ecosystems, and always pack out what you bring in. If you're hiking levada trails, be mindful of narrow walkways and allow faster hikers to pass safely. Some routes involve tunnels, so bringing a reliable headlamp is a simple yet important step in ensuring safe passage through these dark and often wet sections.

14.2 How to Make the Most of Your Hiking Experience

Beyond physical preparation, making the most of your hiking experience in Madeira means fully engaging with the journey, not just the destination. Take the time to absorb your surroundings—the scent of eucalyptus forests, the distant hum of waterfalls, or the sight of a kestrel gliding over deep valleys. Rather than rushing through trails, pause at viewpoints to appreciate the island's dramatic topography, shaped by volcanic activity and erosion over millions of years.

For those seeking solitude, early morning hikes offer the best chance to experience Madeira's trails in their most peaceful state, before the midday crowds arrive. Sunrise hikes to Pico do Arieiro or Pico Ruivo reveal a breathtaking transformation of the landscape as golden light spills over the peaks, making the effort of a pre-dawn start worthwhile. Alternatively, sunset hikes along coastal cliffs, such as Ponta de São Lourenço, cast the rugged coastline in a warm glow, creating a truly unforgettable experience.

Hiking in Madeira is also an opportunity to connect with its rich cultural and natural heritage. Engaging with local guides can offer insights into the history of the levadas, the island's unique flora, and the conservation efforts protecting this remarkable ecosystem. Supporting small businesses, such as local guesthouses or family-run restaurants, also adds depth to your journey, allowing you to experience Madeira not just as a visitor but as part of its vibrant community.

Most importantly, embrace flexibility. Not every hike will go exactly as planned—weather conditions, trail diversions, or unexpected challenges may arise. Being adaptable and approaching each hike with curiosity rather than rigid expectations will lead to a more fulfilling and enriching experience. Madeira's trails have a way of surprising even the most seasoned hikers, revealing new perspectives and hidden wonders along the way.

As you lace up your boots and set off on your adventure, remember that hiking in Madeira is more than just an activity—it's an experience that stays with you long after you've left the island. The memories of towering peaks, mist-filled valleys, and the sheer joy of reaching a summit after a challenging climb will become stories you carry with you, ready to be shared or relived in the future. So, take your time, hike responsibly, and allow the island's breathtaking landscapes to leave their mark on you.

Downloadable Map.

Location of routes and sections.

Happy Hiking!

Printed in Dunstable, United Kingdom

74955123R00060

Tax Planning For Dividends

Lee J Hadnum

IMPORTANT LEGAL NOTICES:

WealthProtectionReportTM
TAX GUIDE - "Tax Planning For Dividends"

Published by:
WealthProtectionReport.co.uk
Email: sales@wealthprotectionreport.co.uk

First Edition: January 2014

Copyright

Copyright © WealthProtectionReport.co.uk All rights reserved.

No part of this publication may be reproduced or transmitted in any form or by any means (electronically or mechanically, including photocopying, recording or storing it in any medium by electronic means) without the prior permission in writing of the copyright owner except in accordance with the provisions of the Copyright, Designs and Patents Act 1988 or under the terms of a licence issued by the Copyright Licensing Agency Ltd, 90 Tottenham Court Road, London, W1P 0LP. All applications for the written permission of the copyright owner to reproduce or transmit any part of this Tax Guide should be sent to the publisher.
Warning: Any unauthorised reproduction or transmission of any part of this Tax Guide may result in criminal prosecution and a civil claim for damages.

Trademarks

The logo "WealthProtectionReportTM" is a trademark of WealthProtectionReport.co.uk. All other logos, trademarks, names and logos in this Tax Guide may be trademarks of their respective owners.

DISCLAIMER

1. Please note that this tax guide is intended as general guidance only for individual readers and does NOT constitute accountancy, tax, legal, investment or other professional advice. WealthProtectionReport and the author accept no responsibility or liability for loss which may arise from reliance on information contained in this tax guide.

2. Please note that tax legislation, the law and practices by government and regulatory authorities (for example, HM Revenue and Customs) are constantly changing and the information contained in this tax guide is only correct as at the date of publication. We therefore recommend that for accountancy, tax, investment or other professional advice, you consult a suitably qualified accountant, tax specialist, independent financial adviser, or other professional adviser. Please also note that your personal circumstances may vary from the general examples given in this tax guide and your professional adviser will be able to give specific advice based on your personal circumstances.

3. This tax guide covers UK taxation mainly and any references to 'tax' or 'taxation' in this tax guide, unless the contrary is expressly stated, are to UK taxation only. Please note that references to the 'UK' do not include the Channel Islands or the Isle of Man. Addressing all foreign tax implications is beyond the scope of this tax guide.

4. Whilst in an effort to be helpful, this tax guide may refer to general guidance on matters other than UK taxation, WealthProtectionReport and the author are not experts in these matters and do not accept any responsibility or liability for loss which may arise from reliance on such information contained in this tax guide.

CONTENTS

1 How Dividends Are Taxed

2 Dividend Splitting

3 Using A Company

4 Using ISA's To Reduce Tax

5 Using Tax Shelters: EIS & VCT's

6 Extracting Dividends Whilst Non UK Resident

7 Tax Treatment Of Foreign Dividends

8 Dividend Waivers

ABOUT THE AUTHOR

Lee Hadnum LLB ACA CTA is an international tax specialist. He is a Chartered Accountant and Chartered Tax Adviser and is the Editor of the popular tax planning website:

www.wealthprotectionreport.co.uk

Lee is also the author of a number of best selling tax planning books including:

- **Tax Planning Techniques Of The Rich & Famous** - Essential reading for anyone who wants to use the same tax planning techniques as the most successful Entrepreneurs, large corporations and celebrities

- **The Worlds Best Tax Havens** – 220 page book looking at the worlds best offshore jurisdictions in detail

- **Non Resident & Offshore Tax Planning –** Offshore tax planning for UK residents or anyone looking to purchase UK property or trade in the UK. A comprehensive guide.

- **Tax Planning With Offshore Companies & Trusts: The A-Z Guide** - Detailed analysis of when and how you can use offshore companies and trusts to reduce your UK taxes

- **Tax Planning For Company Owners** – How company owners can reduce income tax, corporation tax and NICs

- **How To Avoid CGT In 2013/2014** – Tax planning for anyone looking to reduce UK capital gains tax

- **Buy To Let Tax Planning** – How property investors can reduce income tax, CGT and inheritance tax

- **Asset Protection Handbook** – Looks at strategies to ringfence your assets in today's increasing litigious climate

- **Working Overseas Guide** – Comprehensive analysis of how you can save tax when working overseas

- **Double Tax Treaty Planning** – How you can use double tax treaties to reduce UK taxes

1 HOW DIVIDENDS ARE TAXED

The tax treatment of dividends can be extremely confusing because of terms like 'tax credit', 'net dividend' and 'gross dividend'. In reality it's quite simple when you cut through all the jargon. In this chapter we will explain in plain English how dividends are taxed. Then we'll look at some useful tax-planning strategies.

Definitions

Net Dividend

This is the most important dividend number because it is the actual payment you receive from the company whose shares you own. In other words, the cheque you receive is the net dividend.

If you are a higher-rate taxpayer (see Appendix A) you will then have to pay income tax of 25% on this amount. If you have a very high income so that your total income is above £150,000 you would be taxed at 30.55% on the dividend receipt. Basic rate taxpayers would pay no further tax on their dividends.

Gross Dividend

This is calculated by 'grossing up your net dividend'. To do this you multiply the net dividend by 10/9. For example, if your net dividend is £100, the gross dividend is:

£100 x 100/90 = £111.11

This amount is then used when calculating your annual tax bill, as will be shown below.

Tax Credit

When you receive your dividend cheque (your net dividend) it will also detail an amount of 'tax credit'. This is simply 10% of your gross dividend. So if the net dividend is £100 and the gross dividend is £111.11, the dividend tax credit is:

£111.11 x 10% = £11.11

It is important to note that the tax credit cannot be used to create an income tax refund.

Are Gross Dividends and Tax Credits Important?

It's the net dividend that is the most important number for your financial planning because this is the actual income you receive. Gross dividends and tax credits are only important when it comes to doing your paperwork and filling in your tax return.

The Dividend Tax Calculation

Although the 'effective' tax rate for dividends is 30.55% for anyone with income above £150,000, 25% for higher-rate taxpayers and 0% for other taxpayers, the 'formal' tax rates are 37.5%, 32.5% and 10% respectively.

How you arrive at 30.55%, 25% and 0% is by deducting the tax credit when you do your tax calculation. This is best illustrated by means of some examples.

As we've said, when an individual receives a dividend, the amount received is 'grossed up' by the fraction 10/9 and this is known as the gross dividend. The gross dividend is taxed along with the taxpayer's other income.

Example 1 – Basic-rate taxpayer

John receives a £90 dividend. His tax calculation is as follows:

Gross Dividend: £90 x 10/9	£100
Tax @ 10%	£10
Tax credit: £100 x 10%	£10
Tax payable	£0

Example 2 – Higher-rate taxpayer

Jack a higher-rate taxpayer receives a dividend of £90. His tax calculation is as follows:

Gross Dividend: £90 x 10/9		£100
Tax @ 32.5%	£32.50	
Tax credit: £100 x 10%	£10	
Tax payable	£22.5	

Jack has actually received £90. Out of this he will have to pay £22.50 to Revenue and Customs. The effective tax rate is therefore 22.5/90 = 25%.

Example 3 – Additional-rate taxpayer

Denis has income above £150,000 for 2013/2014 and is therefore subject to the new additional rate of tax. He receives a dividend of £90. His tax calculation is as follows:

Gross Dividend: £90 x 10/9		£100
Tax @ 37.5%	£37.50	
Tax credit: £100 x 10%	£10	
Tax payable	£27.5	

Denis has actually received £90. Out of this he will have to pay £27.50 to Revenue and Customs. The effective tax rate is therefore 27.5/90 = 30.55%.

If your dividend income pushes you into the higher-rate tax bracket, your effective tax rate on your dividend income will lie somewhere between 0% and 25%. To see why, it's first important to have a firm grasp of UK income tax rates.

UK Income Tax Rates

For the 2013/2014 tax year the following tax rates apply:

	£
• Savings rate - 10%	2,790
• Basic rate - 20%	32,010
• Higher rate - 40%	150,000
• Additional rate – 45%	Over £150,000

The special savings rate that applies from 6 April 2008 applies only for the purposes of savings income (essentially interest). However, if you have any non savings income (eg salary, profits or rents) that exceed the £2,790 savings band the 10% savings rate would not be available. The interest would then be taxed at the 20% basic rate.

In addition, everyone enjoys a personal allowance of £9,440, which means the first £9,440 of income you receive is completely tax free. What this means is that you only pay tax at 40% when you earn more than £41,450 (£32,010 + £9,440).

It's also important to point out that dividends are the 'top slice' of income so if you earn salary or other income such as rents and interest of more than £41,450, all of your dividends will be taxed at the higher rate. Now let's see how much tax an investor pays who earns all his income from dividends.

Example 1

Phil receives dividends of £45,000 and no other income. How is his tax calculated?

	£
Gross Dividends £45,000 x 100/90	50,000
Less: Personal allowance	9,440
Taxable income	40,560
Tax @ 10% on first £32,010	3,210
Tax @ 32.5% on balance £8,550	2,778.75

Total Tax	5,988.75
Less Tax Credit (10% taxable dividend)	4,056
Tax payable	1,932.75

In total Phil earns £45,000 in dividends and pays tax of £1,933 – an effective tax rate of just over 4%. The tax credit is reduced from £5,000 to £4,056 as part of the dividend is offset by the personal allowance. This restriction usually only applies if there is no other taxable income arising in the year.

This example illustrates that dividends are an extremely tax efficient form of income. What about a taxpayer who earns income from a variety of sources. How much tax would this person end up paying?

Example 2

Pat received the following income during the 2013/14 tax year:

- Salary from employment with Dingbat plc - £20,000
- Rental profits from buy-to-let properties - £8,000
- Bank interest - £2,000 (gross)
- Net dividends from shares in Rich plc - £15,000

Income tax of £3,000 has already been deducted from his salary. His tax bill is calculated as follows:

Salary	£20,000
Rental income	£8,000
Interest	£2,000
Gross Dividends	£16,667
Total taxable income	£46,667
Less: personal allowance	£9,440
	£37,227

Tax on Salary
£20,000 - £9,440 = £10,560 @ 20% £2,112

Rental income
£8,000 @ 20% £1,600

Interest	
£2,000 @ 20%	£400
Dividends	
Balance of basic rate tax band:	
£32,010 – £10,560 – £8,000 – £2,000:	
£11,450 @ 10%	£1,145
Remainder taxed in higher rate band:	
£16,667 - £11,450:	
£5,217 @ 32.5%	£1,696
Total tax	£6,953
Less:	
Tax deducted on interest	£400
PAYE	£3,000
Dividend Tax Credit	£1,667
Total income tax payable	£1,886

In this example, Pat has received dividends totalling £15,000 and paid £1,174 in tax, after subtracting the dividend tax credit. The effective tax rate is just 7.8%.

Remember that dividends are treated as the final source of income when looking at which income to tax first. Therefore if you have dividends and your total income is over the basic rate band (£32,010 for the 2013/14 tax year), some or all of the dividends will be taxed at the higher rate. Once your income exceeds £150,000 you will then be subject to the additional rate of tax (at 45% or 37.5% depending on the type of income).

Payments on Account

Most taxpayers only have to pay income tax on their dividends when they submit their annual tax return. For tax year 2013/2014 if you're filing online you need to file by January 31 following the end of the tax year (31 January 2015 for tax year 2013/2014). If you're filing a paper return you will need to submit it by 31 October 2014 (for the 2013/2014 tax year).

However, if you earn a lot of income from dividends you may have to make two 'payments on account'. These are based on your income tax liability from the previous tax year and have to be paid by 31 January during the tax year and by 31 July following the tax year.

Payments on account are not necessary if:

- Your tax liability for the previous year (net of tax deducted at source) is less than £500, or

- More than 80% of your previous year's tax liability was met by tax deducted at source.

If you have substantial dividend income, or are a share trader, these provisions may therefore apply to you.

Note that interest, which is usually subject to deduction of tax at source, would not be included in assessing whether payments on account are due.

2 DIVIDEND SPLITTING

Spreading ownership of assets between a husband and wife is one of the best ways of avoiding both income tax and capital gains tax. In this section we'll focus on the opportunities to save income tax.

The reason it's possible to split income is that spouses are treated as separate individuals for tax purposes BUT they are allowed to transfer assets between each other with no capital gains tax arising.

To benefit it's important that one of the spouses earns less income than the other. The best case scenario is where one spouse is a higher-rate or additional-rate taxpayer (paying 25%/30.55% tax on dividend income and 40%/45%) and the other spouse earns no income at all.

Remember that, before tax has to be paid at the 45% rate, each UK resident individual is entitled to:

- A personal allowance, currently £9,440.
- A basic rate, currently 20% (0% for dividend income).
- A higher rate, currently 40% (25% for dividend income).

The key is to make sure that your spouse's income tax personal allowance and lower tax rates are fully utilized. In terms of dividends, this can mean the difference between a 25/30.55% effective tax rate and a 0% rate, just by ensuring that shares are owned by the right person at the right time.

In these circumstances, gifting assets to the low-income spouse will reap enormous tax savings. In certain circumstances there will be absolutely no tax payable at all!

Take the example of a married man who has income above £150,000 and who owns shares which generate dividends of £30,000. He would normally pay around £9,165 in income tax. If, however, his wife has no earnings, transferring all of the shares to her would completely eliminate this tax bill.

And remember transferring assets to your spouse has absolutely no capital gains tax consequences.

However, the capital gains tax position would need to be considered when you come to sell the shares. If 100% ownership is transferred to your spouse (rather than, say, 50%) only one capital gains tax exemption will be available when the shares are sold.

In other words, the best split for income tax savings may not be the best split for capital gains tax savings.

However, the good news is that you can have your cake and eat it! There's nothing to stop the lower earning spouse from owning all the shares while they are used to produce dividend income and then transferring 50% (or some other suitable percentage) back to the other spouse prior to sale.

Let's have a look at an example to illustrate the potential benefits.

Example

David has a well paid job in the city and holds share investments that produce net dividend income of £30,000. David will pay income tax of £7,500 on the dividend income as he is a higher- rate taxpayer.

He decides to transfer the shares to his wife, Sue, who earns no other income. She would be entitled to the personal allowance of £9,440 and given that the remaining income falls solely within the basic rate band, the tax credit would cover any income tax liability. She would therefore have no income tax to pay on the £30,000 dividend income. This would be a tax saving for the couple of £7,500, enough to buy a small car!

To do this, 'beneficial title' to the shares must be transferred to the other spouse which some investors may not feel comfortable about.

One option is to make use of the '50:50' rule. Where investment assets are held jointly between husband and wife HMRC automatically assumes that the ownership and hence income is split 50:50, irrespective of the actual split between the spouses. In other words, one spouse can own 99% of the shares and the other spouse can earn 1%, with income split equally for tax purposes.

(This makes the Revenue's job easier as it would be difficult to identify the true beneficial interests in many cases!)

Therefore, even if one owns 1%, and the remaining spouse owns 99% of a shareholding, the income would still be split 50:50.

Where investment assets are held jointly by spouses the 50:50 rule will apply unless the couple make a joint declaration that they want the actual beneficial interests to apply (this can be made on a form 17 - available from the HMRC website).

Clearly, for our share investor who wishes to split income to save tax, without giving away significant title, the answer would be to not make such a declaration.

If 50:50 is not an aggressive enough split, and you want your spouse to be taxed on all the income, it is necessary to transfer beneficial ownership in all the shares.

Although, splitting ownership can result in greater income tax savings, it's important to point out that, if the shares are sold, capital gains tax will follow the actual beneficial interest, and not the 50:50 rule. In other words, all or most of the gains will be taxed in the one spouse's hands.

This could increase the CGT payable because the couple will lose one capital gains tax exemption.

It's also worthwhile noting that the 2004 Budget withdrew the 50:50 rule for shares in close companies. Basically this will apply to unquoted and family companies where the company is controlled by the directors or fewer than five shareholders. In this case, the actual beneficial interests will be used to determine the income for each spouse.

Example

Jack is a higher-rate taxpayer and buys shares worth £100,000. He gifts his wife Emily, who earns no income, a 1% interest in the shares. Dividend income of £15,000 is received during the year.

Assuming no declaration is made by Jack and Emily, the 50:50 rule will apply.

They would each be assessed on income of £7,500, with Jack paying income tax of £1,875 and Emily paying no income tax. Jack has therefore saved himself £1,875 and only transferred 1% of the title.

It would however, be more effective for Jack to transfer all of the shares to his wife. She would then receive the dividends and there would be no income tax payable on the dividends.

However, because only one person owns the shares only one CGT annual exemption will be available when they come to sell.

What Jack and Emily want to do is to minimize both income tax and capital gains tax. To minimize capital gains tax, prior to selling, Emily should transfer sufficient shares so that Jack can make full use of his annual exemption.

For example, let's say Emily holds on to the shares for several years, at which point she decides to take her profits. Let's say the shares have increased in value to £200,000. She is therefore looking at a potential gain of £100,000.

Assuming the annual exemption has risen to £15,000, Emily could transfer shares with a gain equivalent to £15,000 to Jack. This would be equivalent to a transfer of shares with a value of £30,000 (15% of her shareholding).

The remaining 85% would be taxed as follows:

	Jack	Emily

Proceeds	£30,000	£170,000
Less:		
Cost	£15,000	£85,000
Annual exemption	£15,000	£15,000
Taxable Gain	NIL	£80,000

This option would ensure that:

- The ongoing dividend income is taxed at the lowest rate.
- Both annual exemptions are available when the shares are sold.

Although this is perfectly legitimate tax planning, it would be wise not to transfer the interest immediately prior to selling the shares. Although unlikely, HMRC could challenge the transfer in such a circumstance on anti-avoidance grounds. This type of tax planning will therefore work best where the transfer was a suitable period prior to a disposal, and no actions had yet been taken to dispose of the shares.

Beware of a Settlement

One of the main points to watch out for when looking at income splitting opportunities is making sure that you don't get caught by the so-called 'settlement provision's. These are anti-avoidance provisions which have an incredibly wide scope (and that's why it's important to take professional advice). If they apply they could prevent any benefit being obtained from income splitting as dividends received by the 'recipient spouse' would be taxed on the 'gifting spouse'.

One of cases where the settlement provisions could apply is where an individual gifts an asset but retains an interest in the gifted asset.

The settlement provisions do not apply to an outright gift by one spouse to another unless:

- The gift does not carry a right to the whole of the income or
- The property given is wholly or substantially a right to

income.

When you transfer quoted shares to your spouse you'd want to use the exemption for interspouse transfers. This is on the basis that you transferred shares unconditionally and that the shares represented more than 'wholly or substantially' a right to income, as they also represent rights to capital over and voting rights.

The other side of the coin is that the spouse actually making the gift must also not retain an interest in the shares. This would therefore make it vitally important that the transfer was not a 'sham' arrangement and the recipient spouse actually had rights to all the income from the shares, and did not for example pay back dividends to the gifting spouse.

This is one of those areas where it's worthwhile checking with a professional, particularly given HMRC practice in this area can change rapidly.

Using Your Children to Reduce Tax

Once your spouse's personal allowance and lower and basic-rate tax bands are used up, what next? Can you transfer dividend income to your children?

Well, the answer is yes, you can, but unfortunately a transfer of shares to children would be classed as a disposal for capital gains tax purposes, and the disposal proceeds would be deemed to be the market value of the shares. This could result in a hefty capital gains tax bill.

Just as settlement provisions can apply to transfers where a spouse retains an interest, there is also further anti-avoidance legislation that treats income from assets gifted to children as the parent's income when the income exceeds £100.

So, for example, if there is a transfer of shares from a father to his son, the income will be taxed in the son's hands only if it is less than £100 per year. If it's more than that, the whole of the dividend payment will be taxed in the father's hands. Given that he will already have paid capital gains tax on the transfer of the shares, this would be a disastrous state of affairs.

So are there any ways to circumvent these rules? Well, firstly, it only applies to income tax and only where the income is more than £100. So a father could transfer shares which are expected to generate significant capital gains rather than dividend income.

When the children sell the shares the profits will be subject to capital gains tax. However, the potential tax bill could be quite low because children of any age qualify for an annual capital gains tax exemption.

Note that it does not make sense to purchase shares and then transfer them to children, especially if they're showing good profits already as your profits will be subject to capital gains tax.

The best bet would be to consider one of the following strategies:

- Transfer cash to your children so they can buy the shares directly.

- Immediately transfer shares after you have bought them and before any gain arises.

- Purchase the shares purely as a nominee. There would need to be a written agreement substantiating this. Tax would then be payable by the beneficial owner of the shares. As the parent would be the owner of only the legal title to the shares (ie in 'name only'), the gain would be taxed in the hands of the child.

Secondly, it's important to remember that these rules only apply to children under 18 years of age.

If your children are over 18 you can transfer shares to them and the income will be taxed in their hands. Of course, this isn't much use if your children are themselves higher-rate taxpayers. However, a great many parents will be in the situation where their adult children are either studying or, if in work, paying tax at the basic rate. In these circumstances there is scope to save income tax by transferring shares to them.

If your adult children are higher-rate taxpayers but have spouses who earn little or no income, tax savings could be achieved by transferring shares directly to their spouses. Of course this is not always desirable for reasons that have nothing to do with tax.

However, many young couples who earn significantly different amounts of income have very few income-producing assets which allow them to make use of the 'poorer' spouse's personal allowance and basic-rate tax band. This is one way they can.

Remember that you will have to pay capital gains tax on any profits when you make the transfer and so may want to consider following one of the strategies outlined above.

Thirdly, the anti-avoidance rules only apply to parents transferring income-producing assets to their children. They do not apply to grandparents (or uncles and aunts etc) who gift shares to grandchildren.

Note that any gift would need to be a bona fide gift. If the gift was in fact a sham and, for example, the share proceeds were passed pack to the adult who gifted them in the first place, HMRC would argue that the beneficial interest always remained with them and tax accordingly.

Therefore, transfers of shares would be useful for grandparents, in particular, who wish to transfer assets to their grandchildren and reduce their estates for inheritance tax purposes.

Example

Pete and Ethel have three grandchildren. They have a substantial estate, and amongst their various investments have £500,000 invested in an unquoted trading company listed on AIM.

This produces net dividend income of £50,000 per year. As they are both higher-rate taxpayers, the income tax charge would be £12,500.

They decide to transfer the shares to their three grandchildren. They will each receive shares worth £167,667, with annual dividend income of £16,667. As they have no other income they would pay no tax on the dividends.

Note that in this example, unquoted trading shares were used, which we have assumed would enable the shares to qualify for gift relief on the transfer to the grandchildren (see Chapter 23 on inheritance tax planning). If gift relief was not available, this may make the transfer of the shares a no go, given the potential capital gains tax liability that will arise when the shares are transferred.

However all is not lost. If the shares are in a regular quoted company Pete and Ethel could treat the transfer to the grandchildren as more of a long-term exercise and realize just enough profit to make use of their annual capital gains tax exemptions (£20,800 per year).

3 USING A COMPANY TO AVOID TAX ON DIVIDENDS

In certain circumstances using a company could be beneficial to reduce income tax on dividends from a share portfolio.

The reason using a company may be useful from an income tax position is that dividends received by a company from another UK company are usually completely tax free.

The extraction of cash from a share investment company would itself be taxable, and if the cash was extracted as a dividend, there would be no difference between receiving the dividend directly or from your own company.

One long-term strategy could be to use a company as a 'money box' entity. Dividends could be saved up over many years until a sizeable cash balance develops. Let's say you earn £15,000 of dividends per year. After 10 years you will have accumulated £150,000 worth of dividends with a tax saving of about £37,500.

Extraction of the funds in the UK would result in an income tax charge. However the sole shareholder could become non-UK resident and declare a large dividend. As a non-resident individual this would be likely to be 'exempt' from UK income tax with the notional tax credit completely satisfying any income tax liability. Note that after April 2013 you would need to remain non-resident for more than 5 tax years to avoid UK income tax being charged on your return.

The tax saving from using a 'moneybox' company after April 2013 could be even greater if you have other earnings pushing you above £150,000. Using a company to hold the dividends could save you paying income tax at 30.55%.

Problems with Money Box Companies

One of the problems would be finding a country where you want to live and that does not tax the dividends more than in the UK.

In practice, capital gains tax considerations would also be likely to dominate this type of tax planning. For example, by using a UK company the company would remain subject to UK corporation tax, whereas by owning the shares personally, UK CGT could be avoided by becoming non-resident for more than five complete tax years.

There's also the status of the company to consider. The company would need to either be a trading or investment company (or a combination) to gain a deduction for any costs. A passive holding of shares would certainly not qualify as a trading company and would probably not qualify as an investment company either.

Whereas this would not be relevant as regards dividend income of the company (as this would not be taxable), any future gains realized by the company would be taxed in full with no deduction for the expenses of running the company that would ordinarily be available to a trading or investment company.

The Close Investment Company provisions would also apply so any gain would be taxed in the company at a standard 23% (as these provisions do not apply just to investment companies).

Therefore, although a company could be used to mitigate tax on ongoing income, specialist advice would undoubtedly need to be taken and the CGT implications require close inspection.

4 USING ISA'S TO REDUCE TAX

The humble ISA is one of the most powerful tools in the private investor's toolkit. Most couples can invest £23,040 per tax year and shelter all their income and capital gains forever more from the taxman.

However, there's more to ISAs than meets the eye. In this chapter we explain all the rules and, more importantly, show you how ISAs can be utilised to achieve extra tax savings.

Investment Limits

For the 2013/2014 tax year anyone can invest up to £5,760 in a cash ISA. Your maximum ISA limit for this year is £11,520 which means that your ISA share investment can be up to £11,520 (less the amount invested in the cash ISA).

Investors must be aged 18 or over to own share ISAs (16-18 to own cash ISAs).

Investment Options

You can use ISAs to invest in a wide variety of different assets:

- Shares and corporate bonds issued by companies listed on recognised stock exchanges anywhere in the world.

- UK gilts and government bonds issued by other countries in the European Economic Area.

- Units in UK authorised unit trusts or open ended investment companies (OEICs), including property unit trusts.

- Shares in approved investment trusts.

Note that options and warrants cannot be held within an ISA.

Also, only quoted shares can be included. This includes Techmark shares but shares treated as unquoted for tax purposes (for example, shares listed on the Alternative Investment Market) cannot be included within an ISA, unless they are received through a qualifying employee share scheme.

You also cannot put shares you inherit into an ISA or any other existing shares that you already own. There is, however, one exception to this rule. You are allowed to invest certain shares obtained through an employee share scheme.

Losses

Just as any gains from ISA investments are not taxable, so any losses are not available for offset against other gains.

Non-Residency

If you become non resident you are not allowed to continue investing in an ISA. However, HMRC will allow you to keep your ISA investments and they will still obtain the beneficial tax treatment (eg dividends exempt from UK income tax). On your return to the UK, you can then continue to top up your ISA investments.

Using Your Spouse

Spouses are treated independently for tax purposes and therefore each spouse is entitled to invest up to £10,900 per tax year (for the current tax year). This means a married couple can shelter £21,800.

It rarely pays not to use up your ISA allowance as there are generally no penalties, minimum investment periods or other hidden costs.

Using Your Children

There's nothing to stop you gifting cash to your adult children so that they can have their own ISAs. All income and capital gains will be completely tax free.

Remember this could be a potentially exempt transfer for inheritance tax purposes and taxed as part of your estate if you die within seven years. However, the first £3,000 of donations per person per tax year are completely exempt from inheritance tax.

The Benefits of Self-Select ISAs

Self-select ISAs are ideal for active investors. They let you buy and sell shares as often as you like.

They're available from stockbrokers, including online stockbrokers and certain high street banks.

Self-select ISAs are usually more expensive than ordinary ISAs but they've become extremely competitive in recent years and there are some great deals available from some of the online brokers. When choosing a self-select ISA, note the following:

- The cost per trade. These charges have fallen dramatically in recent years. For example, Halifax charges just £11.95 per trade. Some brokers charge less if you make a large number of trades. For example, Barclays currently charges just £6.95 per trade after you've completed 25 trades in a month.

- Admin charge. Some brokers such as Alliance Trust do not levy any annual fee. Others such as SelfTrade charge a flat fee of £12.50 per year and others such as Halifax charge a percentage, typically .05% per month (with a maximum of £8.33 per month).

- Investment choice. Some self-select ISAs offer a bigger range of shares and investment funds than others. For example, some offer foreign stocks, others don't.

- Exit penalties. If you wish to switch to a new ISA there may be an exit charge. It's advisable to check up on this before you open a self-select ISA. It's only after you open an account that you will discover what quality of service is provided so it is advisable to keep your options open.

- Efficiency. Competitive charges are only one side of the coin. You also have to have faith in the firm's ability to handle your trades quickly and efficiently.

Self-select ISAs are available from many stockbrokers and certain high street banks and other financial companies:

- Halifax - www.halifax.co.uk/sharedealing
- Barclays - www.stockbrokers.barclays.co.uk
- Killik & Co - www.killikisa.co.uk
- Hargreaves Lansdown - www.h-l.co.uk
- Selftrade - www.selftrade.co.uk
- Alliance Trust – www.alliancetrusts.comTax Tip

So should you use a self-select ISA? Naturally, if all you do is trade shares a self-select ISA is essential. But what if you regularly trade shares and also have long-term holdings – should you use your ISA allowance to protect your long-term investments or your short-term trades?

The answer depends critically on whether your annual trading profits currently exceed your annual CGT exemption (£10,900 if you're single, £21,800 if you're married).

If they do, then it almost certainly pays to use a self-select ISA for trading purposes and invest your long–term holdings directly in shares or unit trusts.
Why? Because if your annual trading profits exceed the CGT exemption they will definitely be taxed. By its very nature 'trading' means you are making disposals which give rise to CGT. But tax will be completely avoided on capital that is sheltered by a self-select ISA.

In contrast, if your 'paper' profits from your long-term holdings exceed the annual CGT exemption they will not be taxed until you make a disposal, with the annual capital gains tax exemption then being offset.

What if your annual trading profits do not exceed your annual

CGT exemption?

If you trade through an ISA and your profits are less than £10,900 (£21,800 if married) you will not receive any immediate tax benefit because your profits are already tax free. However, if you enjoy success and your profits grow you will eventually pay CGT so an ISA is arguably still worth considering. Your long-term holdings will then be invested directly but again will not be subject to CGT until you sell, by which time they could be covered by the annual CGT allowance.

The only drawback with using a self-select ISA as a frequent trader is that you are limited to the amount of capital you can invest. If you have a substantial trading portfolio you will then end up with some of your trades done through an ISA and the others done directly. This could result in multiple orders, possibly with multiple brokers and may be more trouble than it's worth. In these cases, especially if your profits are well below the annual CGT exemption, it may be worth using an ISA to protect your long-term investments.

Equities vs Bonds

If you have a balanced portfolio with some of your money in shares and the rest in gilts and corporate bonds, it may be worth considering whether it's your bonds or your shares that are sheltered in ISAs. Because most of the return from bonds comes in the form of taxable interest, it probably makes sense to use an ISA to protect these investments rather than shares. Equity returns, on the other hand, come mainly in the form of capital growth which qualifies for the annual CGT exemption and the 18%/28% rate of capital gains tax.

You should arguably only use your ISA allowance to shelter equities if you expect them to generate significantly higher returns than your bonds over time.

How Should You Use Your ISA Savings?

Some investors use ISAs to save for a specific eventuality, such as paying for a child's education. This is arguably not a good idea because once you sell your ISAs the tax benefits are lost forever.

If you're saving to pay for a future expense there's a very good chance that by investing directly in equities or unit trusts, rather than using an ISA wrapper, you will pay little or no capital gains tax anyway, leaving your precious ISA allowance free to put to better uses.

Example 1

Dave and Sue inherit £20,000 and decide to invest in an equity unit trust (note, not an ISA) for 10 years. After that they intend to use most of the funds to pay for their children's education. They enjoy annual returns of 7% per year. After 10 years the fund will be worth £39,343 with a total profit of £19,343. How much tax will they pay?

It is unlikely that they would pay any tax as the gain of £19,343 would be covered by their two annual CGT exemptions.

So even though Dave and Sue invested a sizeable chunk of money and earned a respectable return, they did not pay a penny in tax on their profits. If Dave and Sue had used an ISA instead they would have derived absolutely no tax benefit.

Where ISAs really come into their own is where you hold on to them for many years and use them to generate tax-free income when you retire.

Example 2

Dave and Sue decide to invest their £28,000 in an ISA for a period of 20 years to fund their retirements. Based on the same growth assumptions as the previous example, after 20 years the investment will be worth £108,351. They now wish to retire and switch from a growth fund to an income-focused fund (ISA supermarkets, for example, allow you to invest in different funds provided by different managers and switch from one to the other). The income fund has a yield of 6%, delivering them a tax-free income of £6,501 per year.

If instead of using an ISA Dave and Sue had invested directly the outcome would be entirely different. First of all the switch from a growth fund to an income fund would result in a capital gains tax charge (in this case £9,063 assuming an annual exemption of £15,000). This means they have less capital to invest for income and so their income will be just £5,957.

However that's not the end of the story. There's still tax to pay on this income. Assuming half comes from share dividends and half comes from bond interest if they are higher rate taxpayers their after-tax income will be just £4,021.

Hence by using an ISA they end up with 62% more income than by investing directly in unit trusts.
The important lessons to learn from this example are that:

- ISAs allow you, in certain circumstances, to switch between different investment funds without paying any tax. This is very valuable if you want to rebalance your portfolio every now and again.

- ISAs are most effective when held for the long term with a view to ultimately generating income.

5 USING TAX SHELTERS: EIS & VCT SHARES

A tax shelter is an investment that offers favourable tax treatment, either by allowing you to defer or avoid tax. They're often established by Governments to encourage funds to be invested in higher risk activities that wouldn't normally attract the average investor. The two best-known tax shelters for UK investors are:

- Enterprise Investment Scheme (EIS) shares.
- Venture Capital Trusts (VCTs).

Enterprise Investment Scheme (EIS) Shares

The EIS scheme offers two significant forms of tax relief: income tax relief and capital gains tax relief.

Income Tax Relief

This allows an EIS investor to obtain an income tax credit for the 2013/2014 tax year equal to 30% of the amount invested.

The maximum investment that qualifies is £1,000,000.

This means that income tax relief at 30% can be obtained on investments of up to £1,000,000 provided you have a large income tax liability to utilise all the relief (as an income tax loss cannot be created).

Example

Johnny purchases qualifying EIS shares for £60,000. His income tax bill for the year is £22,000. He will obtain income tax relief equal to £18,000 (£60,000 x 30%). He will therefore only pay £4,000 in income tax.

Capital Gains Tax Relief

Enterprise Investment Schemes offer the following capital gains tax breaks:

- Capital gains from the sale of other assets (eg other shares or property) can be held over against qualifying EIS shares purchased up to one year prior to the disposal and three years after.

- Any capital gain arising when the EIS shares are sold is not taxable provided income tax relief has been given and not withdrawn and the shares are held for a qualifying period, which is usually three years.

Example

Peter makes a gain of £75,000 after selling shares in Lucky plc, a major quoted company and is concerned about his CGT exposure.

If he was to invest £75,000 in qualifying EIS shares within three years of making the sale capital gains tax will be deferred on the £75,000 until the earliest of the following:

- The disposal of the EIS shares (excluding a disposal to a spouse)
- Peter ceases to be UK resident
- The company ceases to be a qualifying EIS company

In addition the taxpayer can claim a lesser amount of relief. So, in the above example, if the disposal occurred in tax year 2013/2014 Peter could have claimed deferral relief of £64,100.

This would then leave a gain of £10,900 chargeable which, if no other gains existed during the tax year, would be fully offset by the annual exemption.

These reliefs sound very attractive. The problem is that they can be very restrictive and although a full analysis of the details of the EIS scheme is outside the scope of this book, it is important to note that EIS tax breaks only apply to 'qualifying' companies which essentially means that the company must be an unquoted trading company that falls within a list of approved trades.

Shares traded on the Alternative Investment Market are regarded as unquoted for this purpose and for share investors it is likely to be only AIM shares that have the potential to qualify under the EIS scheme.

If you are interested in exploring the opportunities available under the EIS scheme, it is important to obtain professional advice.

Venture Capital Trusts (VCTs)

Venture capital trusts were introduced to encourage individuals to invest in unquoted trading companies. Normally the VCT will be a quoted fund that invests in unquoted companies. VCTs offer a variety of generous tax breaks designed to offset the risks inherent in such companies:

- Dividends are completely tax free.

- Share subscribers (in other words, those who invest in the fund when it issues new shares) can obtain income tax relief equivalent to 30% of the amount invested, up to a maximum of £200,000.

- There is no capital gains tax when you sell your VCT shares.

- The VCT itself does not pay tax when it sells qualifying shares. This leaves more proceeds to distribute in the form of a tax-free dividend.

On the downside, the 2004 Budget prevented capital gains tax holdover relief from applying on these investments from 6th April 2004. Therefore unlike investments in EIS shares, you can't defer existing capital gains by investing in a VCT.
Income Tax Relief

Subscribers to new VCT shares are entitled to 30% income tax relief on investments of up to £200,000 per year.

To prevent this relief being taken away, the VCT shares must be held onto for at least five years if you buy them after 6 April 2006 (three

years if you bought them between 6 April 2000 and 5 April 2006).
It's standard practice for the VCT to give investors a certificate which can be used to claim tax relief. This can be done by obtaining an adjustment to your PAYE tax coding from HMRC or by waiting until you submit your tax return.
Example

Jack earns a £200,000 bonus during the 2013/2014 tax year on which he expects to pay 45% tax amounting to £90,000.

To reduce his tax bill Jack invests the maximum £200,000 in a newly launched VCT.

He will be entitled to a tax credit equal to 30% x £200,000 = £60,000, thereby reducing tax on the bonus to £30,000.

(Note: If Jack's expected income tax liability was just £50,000, the £60,000 credit would reduce his income tax liability to zero but would not create a repayment of income tax.)

The Risks

In the above example Jack has generated a £60,000 tax saving but he ends up with £200,000 worth of venture capital trust shares which he has to hold on to for at least five years.

That may not be a bad thing: the shares might rocket in value... but they may also become almost worthless if the trust makes disastrous investment choices.

For example, if in three years' time the shares have fallen by more than 30%, Jack will be worse off than if he had just paid the full tax on his bonus.

Although the firms promoting these investments would argue to the contrary, venture capital trusts are much more risky than most other share investments... why else do you think the Government uses tax relief to encourage people to invest in them?

Nevertheless the income tax credit provides a massive cushion against any price fall and, with expert advice on which VCT to invest in, Jack could end up with a very profitable and tax-efficient investment.

Capital Gains Tax Relief

If Jack's shares have risen in value he will enjoy a further benefit: the gain will be completely tax free. Venture capital trust profits are exempt from capital gains tax.

In the same vein, however, no relief is available for capital losses.

The capital gains deferral provisions no longer apply, so you can no longer roll over capital gains from selling other shares or property investments by investing in a VCT.

Revenue and Customs has detailed rules that need to be satisfied by a VCT in order for investors to qualify for the various tax breaks. It is not necessary to examine the rules here but it is important to be aware of them.

6 EXTRACTING DIVIDENDS WHILST NON UK RESIDENT

There is no withholding tax on UK dividends paid overseas, and for UK tax purposes, there will be no higher rate income tax charge.

All dividends are treated as having been subject to a 10% tax charge at source and for non-UK residents, this will satisfy any basic rate income tax liability, so effectively dividend income is tax free in your hands if your non UK resident.

Just as for UK residents, the 10% 'deemed' tax credit cannot give rise to a repayment of income tax

However, depending on the terms of any double taxation agreement, income tax may STILL be payable in the home country

New Temporary Non Resident Rules

For periods before 6 April 2013 there was nothing to stop you becoming non resident for a single tax year and receiving many forms of UK income free of UK tax.

In fact, extracting dividends during a complete tax year of non residence was often a good tax planning option.

Aside from "offshore income gains" many forms of income as described in the previous chapter could be received free of UK tax. Note for offshore income gains (which taxes gains from offshore funds as income) provisions were introduced from 1 December 2009 to apply a 5 year non residence requirement

However, with the new Statutory Residence Test which applies from 6 April 2013, the Government are also bringing in some new provisions to target short periods of residence where there is an extraction of UK income.

New anti avoidance rules known as the "Temporary Non Residence Provisions" will apply to:

• Dividends and other income from closely controlled companies (but only where the income is derived from profits which arose before departure).

• Lump sum benefits from flexible drawdowns and from Employer-Financed Retirement Benefits Schemes (EFRBS).

• Chargeable event gains on life assurance contracts.

The provisions will NOT apply to:

- Employment income,
- Interest on savings
- Most forms of pension income (annuities, capped drawdown)
- Self-employment
- Dividends from listed companies

What do the provisions say?

The new anti avoidance rules state that if during your period of temporary non residence you receive a dividend (or realise a chargeable event/receive a pension lump sum etc as above) the dividend (or other income) is taxed in the tax year of your return to the UK.

So if you own the shares in a UK company which has significant profits and you become non resident for a temporary period and extract the cash/profits as dividends, whilst no tax will be charged on the dividends
in the tax year of non residence, when you return to the UK you will then be subject to income tax on the dividend.

Important points

There are a couple of crucial points as to how these provisions apply.

1. **Post departure profits**

In the case of dividends they only apply to dividends from "post-departure trade profits."

These are defined as:

(a) trade profits of the company arising in an accounting period that begins after the start of the temporary period of non residence, and

(b) so much of any trade profits of the company arising in an accounting period that straddles the start of that temporary period as is attributable (on a just and reasonable basis) to a time after the start of that temporary period.

The extent to which a dividend is paid in respect of post-departure trade profits is to be determined on a just and reasonable basis.

This therefore protects profits of the company that are made after you actually leave the UK. You can then extract them as dividends free of UK tax when you're non resident even if you're only non resident for a couple of years.

2. Meaning of temporarily non-resident

An individual is treated as "temporarily non-resident" if they meet the following conditions:

□ he or she is UK resident for a tax year and, immediately following that year one or more tax years occur where the individual is not UK resident.

□ In 4 or more tax years out of the 7 tax years immediately preceding the year of departure the individual must be UK resident or the year must
have been a split year that included a period when the individual was UK resident.

□ The temporary period of non-residence must be 5
years or less.

This last point is important as it represents a change from the current CGT provisions which apply if there are fewer than five tax years between the year of departure and the year of return.

So from April 2013 you will need to ensure that you remain non resident for at least six complete tax years if you want to avoid the temporary non resident provisions.

However the latest legislation currently states:

"...Part 4 of this Schedule has effect if the year of departure (as defined in that Part) is the tax year 2013-14 or a subsequent tax year..."

Therefore these temporary non resident provisions will only apply where your period of departure is on or after 6 April 2013.

If you are non resident before that date none of the above provisions should apply to you.

7 TAX TREATMENT OF FOREIGN DIVIDENDS

As we've seen in an earlier chapter, dividends from UK companies are taxed at 10%, 32.5% and 42.5%. However as there is a 1/9 tax credit available the effective tax rates are 0%, 25% and 36.1% Therefore any dividends would not suffer additional tax until the basic rate band was exceeded.

If you receive dividends from overseas you would usually still be taxed at the 10%/32.5%/42.5%.

In the 2007 Budget it was announced that, from 6th April 2008, a UK resident who receives dividends from an offshore company can reclaim the 10% 'deemed' tax credit. For the 2008 tax year this is restricted as it will only apply where a person owns less than 10% of the offshore company.

However, these restrictions are removed for dividends received after 22 April 2009. Therefore any overseas dividends received by a UK resident will be entitled to the 10% deemed tax credit (providing the company is subject to overseas corporation tax).

As such there would be no additional income tax due until the higher rate tax band was exceeded. The new rules mean that basic rate taxpayers will not have to pay any income tax on overseas dividends.

Choice between the Remittance and Arising Basis

Non-doms must make a choice every year between the remittance basis and the arising basis.

Under the remittance basis you qualify for special tax treatment if you decide to keep your income and gains overseas. The arising basis is the way most UK residents are taxed and means you pay tax immediately, regardless of whether you keep the money overseas or bring it into the UK.

In the past, non-doms were automatically taxed on the remittance basis in some cases. Now you'll have to actively claim to be taxed this way. If you don't, you'll automatically be taxed on the arising basis.

Because they can make a different choice every year, non-doms have flexibility to do some constructive tax planning.

Special Concession

The new rules contain one very important concession for the first chunk of overseas income you earn. If your unremitted income and gains are less than £2,000, the remittance basis applies automatically.

If you keep within this limit you effectively 'fall under the radar' and your overseas income and gains can be kept offshore and tax free. Note that for your tax return you will, however, need to tick boxes 27 and 28 of the remittance pages to take advantage of this special rule.

If you are a higher-rate taxpayer, this concession could save you £799.60 in tax every year:

£1,999 x 40% tax = £799.60

And if you are married and your spouse is also non-domiciled the total potential tax saving is £1,599:

£1,999 x 2 x 40% = £1,599

You'll notice we use the number £1,999. That's because your unremitted overseas income must be less than £2,000. If you have £2,000 or more of unremitted income, you do not qualify at all for this concession.

The concession is more generous than it appears. A non-dom who earns, say, 3% interest can effectively keep around £65,000 offshore and out of the UK taxman's clutches. A married couple who are both non-domiciled can keep almost £130,000 offshore and not worry about UK tax.

You can get your hands on these tax savings by simply spending the money when you travel abroad or taking advantage of any of the provisions for "exempt" remittances.

Everyone Qualifies for the Exemption

It's important to point out that you can benefit from this concession even if your total overseas income exceeds £1,999.

What matters is how much "unremitted overseas income" you have, not your total overseas income.

So as long as you remit the rest of your income and gains to the UK and pay tax you will still qualify.

For example, if you earn £10,000 overseas interest during the year, you can remit £8,001 to the UK and pay tax on it and keep £1,999 offshore and tax free.

It's also important to point out that all non-doms qualify for this concession, no matter how long they've lived in the UK.

Other non-dom tax concessions are taken away after you've been living in the UK for a certain length of time.

The 2009 Budget further extended the provisions to ensure that the remittance basis applies automatically where a non-dom has total UK income or gains of no more than £100 which have been taxed in the UK, provided they make no remittances to the UK during the tax year.

Watch Our For Foreign Dividends

The above applies to foreign interest of a non UK domiciliary.

If a non UK domiciliary receives dividends they should carefully consider the impact of a change in the tax rate on those dividends if they claim the remittance basis.

This is important as the tax rate that a UK resident, non domiciliary will pay on their foreign dividends will depend on whether they opt for the arising basis or the remittance basis.

Tax rates on foreign dividends if the Arising basis is chosen:

Basic rate band - 10%

Higher rate band – 32.5%

Additional rate band – 37.5%

Tax rates on foreign dividends if the Remittance basis is chosen:

Basic rate band - 20%

Higher rate band – 40%

Additional rate band – 45%

If you are taxed on the remittance basis you are liable to UK tax on dividends paid by foreign companies that are 'remitted to the UK' at the normal tax rates (currently 20 per cent, 40 per cent and 45 per cent) and not at the special rates applicable to dividends (currently 10 per cent, 32.5 per cent and 37.5 per cent).

This means that opting for the remittance basis of tax can have a big impact on your UK tax on foreign dividends as your tax rate can increase significantly.

As such it may not be attractive to opt for the remittance basis of tax if your unremitted income is less than £2,000 if you have foreign dividend income.

8 DIVIDEND WAIVERS

A dividend waiver involves a shareholder not accepting part of a dividend declared.

If therefore shares were held 75/25 a £1,000 dividend would usually be split £750/£250. However if the shareholders wanted to arrange for an equal split the first shareholder could waive £500 of the dividend leaving a dividend of £250 each.

There are a lot of reasons why making a dividend waiver can be attractive but it's often to do with avoiding tax at the higher/additional rate and making the most of someones basic rate tax band.

The main risk when a dividend waiver is used is that the settlements provisions would apply and the dividend would be taxed on the basis of the actual shareholding.

The Revenue state that the factors that may indicate that the Settlements legislation could apply include:

•The level of retained profits, including the retained profits of subsidiary companies, being insufficient to allow the same rate of dividend to be paid on all issued share capital.

•Although there are sufficient retained profits to pay the same rate of dividend per share for the year in question, there has been a succession of waivers over several years where the total dividends payable in the absence of the waivers exceed accumulated realised profits.

•There is any other evidence, which suggests that the same rate would not have been paid on all the issued shares in the absence of the waiver.

•The non-waiving shareholders are persons whom the waiving shareholder can reasonably be regarded as wishing to benefit by the waiver.

•The non-waiving shareholder would pay less tax on the dividend than the waiving shareholder.

The main risk in many cases would be that there would be insufficient profits to pay the rate of dividend for all of the shares. You would therefore need to carefully consider this and if it did apply you would be classed as making a settlement.

If a settlement existed the dividend waiver would effectively be ignored and the dividend waived would be taxed on the first shareholder.

Private arrangement

Another option would be to declare a dividend and for the shareholders to account privately for the transfer of funds .

Example

If shares are held 75/25 but an equal cash extraction is required a dividend of £3,750 to one and £1,250 to the other could be made which would be assessed as such for tax purposes.

Then a private informal arrangement for the cash to be transferred from one to the other could be made. This should not be taxed on the recipient, given it would have already have been taxed. You'd need to assess the impact on the rate of tax though. If both were higher rate taxpayers there may not be an issue.

Sample Dividend Waiver

If you're interested in using a dividend waiver, we've you should be looking to evidence it by something similar to this:

I, XXXX{NAME}, of XXXX{ADDRESS} the registered holder of X{NUMBER OF SHARES} Ordinary shares of £X{NOMINAL VALUE OF SHARES} each in the capital of XXXXX LIMITED {COMPANY NAME} (hereinafter called "the company") HEREBY:-

1) Waive all right to participate by reason of X{NUMBER OF

SHARES} of my said Ordinary shares in any XXXX{INTERIM/FINAL} dividend which might be declared or paid by the Company during the period XXXXX {DATE OF DIVIDEND PAYMENT} for its trading year ending XXXX {COMPANY ACCOUNTING PERIOD}.

2) Release unto the Company all such monies as I may become entitled to by way of such dividend referable to my said shares.

DATED the day of Two thousand and eight

IN WITNESS whereof I have hereunto set my hand

SIGNED AND DELIVERED AS A DEED by the said

in the presence of

Witness Address

ABOUT THE AUTHOR

Lee Hadnum LLB ACA CTA is an international tax specialist. He is a Chartered Accountant and Chartered Tax Adviser and is the Editor of the popular tax planning website:

www.wealthprotectionreport.co.uk

Lee is also the author of a number of best selling tax planning books.

OTHER TAX GUIDES

- **Tax Planning Techniques Of The Rich & Famous** - Essential reading for anyone who wants to use the same tax planning techniques as the most successful Entrepreneurs, large corporations and celebrities
- **The Worlds Best Tax Havens** – 220 page book looking at the worlds best offshore jurisdictions in detail
- **Non Resident & Offshore Tax Planning –** Offshore tax planning for UK residents or anyone looking to purchase UK property or trade in the UK. A comprehensive guide.
- **Tax Planning With Offshore Companies & Trusts: The A-Z Guide** - Detailed analysis of when and how you can use offshore companies and trusts to reduce your UK taxes
- **Tax Planning For Company Owners** – How company owners can reduce income tax, corporation tax and NICs
- **How To Avoid CGT In 2013/2014** – Tax planning for anyone looking to reduce UK capital gains tax
- **Buy To Let Tax Planning** – How property investors can reduce income tax, CGT and inheritance tax
- **Asset Protection Handbook** – Looks at strategies to ringfence your assets in today's increasing litigious climate
- **Working Overseas Guide** – Comprehensive analysis of how you can save tax when working overseas
- **Double Tax Treaty Planning** – How you can use double tax treaties to reduce UK taxes

Printed in Great Britain
by Amazon

33080315R00033